ECDL Module 3:
Word Processing

Springer
London
Berlin
Heidelberg
New York
Barcelona
Hong Kong
Milan
Paris
Singapore
Tokyo

ICDL Approved Courseware
Syllabus Version 3.0

ECDL Approved Courseware
Syllabus Version 3.0

ECDL Module 3:
Word Processing
ECDL – the European PC standard

by **David Penfold**

Springer

BCS

LONDON BOROUGH OF BARKING & DAGENHAM	
000832263 CH	
H J	26/03/2001
001.6424 ECD	✓
WHALEBONE	

The Publisher and the BCS would like to publicly acknowledge the vital support of the ECDL Foundation in validating and approving this book for the purpose of studying for the European-wide ECDL qualification.

Springer-Verlag London Ltd, Sweetapple House, Catteshall Road, Godalming, Surrey GU7 3DJ or

The British Computer Society, 1 Sanford Street, Swindon, Wiltshire SN1 1HJ

ISBN 1-85233-444-4

British Library Cataloguing in Publication Data
Penfold, David
   ECDL module 3: word processing: ECDL – the European PC standard. – (European computer driving licence)
   1. Microsoft Word 97 (Computer file)
   I. Title
   652.5'5369

   ISBN 1852334444

The use of registered names, trademarks etc. in this publication does not imply, even in the absence of a specific statement, that such names are exempt from the relevant laws and regulations and are therefore free for general use.

Disclaimer
Although every care has been taken by the author, the British Computer Society and the Publisher in the preparation of this publication, no warranty is given by the author, the British Computer Society and the Publisher as to the accuracy or completeness of the information contained within it and neither the author, the British Computer Society nor the Publisher shall be responsible or liable for any errors or omissions.

Printed and bound at The Cromwell Press, Trowbridge, Wiltshire, England.
34/3830-543210 Printed on acid-free paper SPIN 10792502

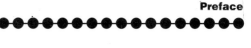

Preface

This book is intended to help you successfully complete the test for Module 3 of the European Computer Driving Licence (ECDL). However before we start working through the actual content of the guide you may find it useful to know a little bit more about the ECDL in general and where this particular Module fits into the overall framework.

What Is The ECDL?

The European Computer Driving Licence (ECDL) is a European-wide qualification that enables people to demonstrate their competence in computer skills. It certifies the candidate's knowledge and competence in personal computer usage at a basic level and is based upon a single agreed syllabus.

This syllabus covers a range of specific knowledge areas and skill sets, which are broken down into seven modules. Each of the modules must be passed before the ECDL certificate can be awarded, though they may be taken in any order but must be completed within a three year period.

Testing of candidates is at audited testing centres, and successful completion of the test will demonstrate the holder's basic knowledge and competence in using a personal computer and common computer applications.

The implementation of the ECDL in the UK is being managed by the British Computer Society. It is growing at a tremendous rate and is set to become the most widely recognised qualification in the field of work-related computer use.

The ECDL Modules

The seven modules which make up the ECDL certificate are described briefly below:

Module 1: Basic Concepts of Information Technology covers the physical make-up of a personal computer and some of the basic concepts of Information Technology such as data storage and memory, and the uses of information networks within computing. It also looks at the application of computer software in society and the use of IT systems in everyday situations. Some basic security and legal issues are also addressed.

Module 2: Using the Computer and Managing Files covers the basic functions of a personal computer and its operating system. In particular it looks at operating effectively within the desktop environment, managing and organising files and directories, and working with desktop icons.

Module 3: Word Processing covers the use of a word processing application on a personal computer. It looks at the basic operations associated with creating, formatting and finishing a word processing document ready for distribution. It also addresses some of the more advanced features such as creating standard tables, using pictures and images within a document, importing objects and using mail merge tools.

Module 4: Spreadsheets covers the basic concepts of spreadsheets and the ability to use a spreadsheet application on a personal computer. Included are the basic operations for developing, formatting and using a spreadsheet, together with the use of basic formulas and functions to carry out standard mathematical and logical operations. Importing objects and creating graphs and charts are also covered.

Module 5: Database covers the basic concepts of databases and the ability to use a database on a personal computer. It addresses the design and planning of a simple database, and the retrieval of information from a database through the use of query, select and sort tools.

Module 6: Presentation covers the use of presentation tools on a personal computer, in particular creating, formatting and preparing presentations. The requirement to create a variety of presentations for different audiences and situations is also addressed.

Module 7: Information and Communication is divided into two main sections, the first of which covers basic Web search tasks using a Web browser and search engine tools. The second section addresses the use of electronic mail software to send and receive messages, to attach documents, and to organise and manage message folders and directories.

This guide focuses upon Module 3.

How To Use This Guide

The purpose of this guide is to take you through all of the knowledge areas and skill sets specified in the syllabus for Module 3. The use of clear, non technical explanations and self paced exercises will provide you with an understanding of the key elements of the syllabus and give you a solid foundation for moving on to take the ECDL test relating to this Module. All exercises contained within this guide are based upon the Windows 98 operating system and Office 97 software.

ECDL

Each chapter has a well defined set of objectives that relate directly to the syllabus for the ECDL Module 3. Because the guide is structured in a logical sequence you are advised to work through the chapters one at a time from the beginning. Throughout each chapter there are various review questions so that you can determine whether you have understood the principles involved correctly prior to moving on to the next step.

Conventions Used In This Guide

Throughout this guide you will come across notes alongside a number of icons. They are all designed to provide you with specific information related to the section of the book you are currently working through. The icons and the particular types of information they relate to are as follows:

Additional Information: Further information or explanation about a specific point.

Caution: A word of warning about the risks associated with a particular action, together with guidance, where necessary on how to avoid any pitfalls.

Definition: A plain English definition of a newly introduced term or concept.

Short Cuts: Short cuts and hints for using a particular program more effectively.

As you are working through the various exercises contained within this guide, you will be asked to carry out a variety of actions:

● Where we refer to commands or items that you are required to select from the PC screen, then we indicate these in bold, for example: Click on the **Yes** button.
● Where you are asked to key text in to the PC, then we indicate this in italics, for example: Type in the words '*Saving my work*'.

You should now be in a position to use this guide, so lets get started. Good luck!

Contents

★ ECDL ★

★ ECDL ★

1

Introduction

In this chapter we will cover

- *What word processing is.*
- *What is meant by formatting.*
- *Which word processor we will use as the basis of the content for this book.*
- *An outline of the book.*

★ ECDL ★

1.1. What is a Word Processor?

A word processor is a computer program that allows you to enter text and edit it. In addition, you can format the text in various ways and include pictures and tables, so that, once all the processing is complete, you obtain a document that is laid out in the way that you wish. This may be a simple letter or it may be the chapter of a book, although some of the more advanced techniques required for the latter may be beyond the scope of this guide.

1.2. What is Formatting?

In Module 2 of this series, you saw how a text editor can be used to input and edit text, that is, words made up of letters and spaces. Figure 1.1 shows a screen shot of a text editor. In the screen shot you can see that text looks as though it has been typed on an old-fashioned typewriter; this is called the Courier typeface, which has been set as the default. Note that any other typeface stored on your computer could have been used instead, but when the text file is saved (usually with a file extension .txt, e.g. yourfile.txt), it is only the letters and spaces (plus a few characters such as the tab and the carriage return) that are saved. There is no formatting.

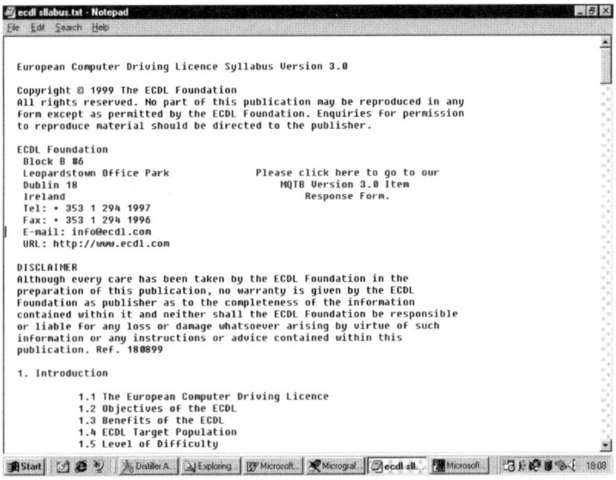

Figure 1.1 The Notepad (text editor) window.

With a word processor, the situation is different. You can define the typeface, or typefaces, you want to use, the typesizes to be used, the interline spacing, the interparagraph spacing, indents, alignment (left, right or centre) and a large number of other parameters. When you save the file (with the extension .doc, e.g. myfile.doc), all these parameters are saved too, unlike with a simple text editor.

You can even group all these changes together to form a style, to which you can give a name and, in turn you can group these styles, together with other details such as the page layout, into a template, which you can save as a special kind of file and use again to provide a structure for other documents.

1.3. Which Word Processor?

This book is about Word 97, the version of Microsoft Word that forms part of Office 97, but there are other word processors as well. There are earlier versions of Word (and sometimes it is useful to save in an earlier format, such as Word 6, if you are sending your file to someone else), there is the more recent Word 2000, which is still very new, and there is Word 98, which is the version of Word 97 that runs on an Apple Macintosh. There are also word processors provided by other software suppliers. Probably the most widely used on the PC platform are Corel WordPerfect and WordPro (previously called AmiPro), which forms part of the Lotus SmartSuite. Although some of the commands are different in these programs, in general they can be used to achieve the same effects as Word 97 and, if you follow and understand the chapters in this guide, you should be able to use any other word processor without too much difficulty, particularly if you use the Help files intelligently.

1.4. Outline of the Book

In Chapter 2, we look at the first steps in word processing, such as how to open and close Word 97, how to open, edit and save a document, how to create a new document and how to use the Help functions.

In Chapter 3 we see how to change the basic settings, in other words, how to look at the document in different ways, as a basic series of lines, as pages, as a World Wide Web document or even just the outline of the document. We shall also see how you can change the page magnification and modify the toolbars, which contain icons for many of the formatting and other operations.

Chapter 4 deals with how to save the document in other formats. These include as a simple text file, other versions of Word, other word processor formats and as what is called Rich Text Format (RTF), which is a text file in which all the formatting commands can be seen as codes. We shall also see how to save a document in a form that can be loaded onto the World Wide Web. This is also a text file with the formatting commands included in a language called HTML (HyperText Markup Language).

In the next few chapters we shall look at basic editing operations. Chapter 5 covers how to insert and delete characters, words, sentences, paragraphs and special characters, such as accents, fixed spaces and mathematical symbols. We shall also see how to insert a page break and, very importantly, how to use the undo command, which allows you cancel not just the last change you made, but a whole series of changes, one by one or all together. Chapter 6 covers how to select characters, words, sentences, paragraphs or even the whole document. We shall also see how to move or copy the selected text, not just within a single document, but between open documents and even into and from other open applications, and finally how to delete sections of text. Chapter 7 covers searching for characters within a document and how to replace them with other characters.

The following chapters then cover formatting. Chapter 8 is about how to change the attributes of the text (typefaces and type sizes – also known as fonts – both the typeface itself and the size, italic, bold and underlines, the colour, the alignment). We shall also see how to use hyphenation if appropriate, how to indent, change the line spacing and copy the formatting from a selected piece of text. Chapter 9 is concerned with tabs, how to use them and how to set them. We also look at adding borders to your document and using lists. Chapter 10 is concerned with styles and templates. Chapter 11 explains how to add page numbering. We shall also see how to add more complex headers and footers and how to insert the date, page numbers and other information in either of these, as well as how to format them.

Chapter 12 shows you how to check spelling and grammar, making changes where necessary, while Chapter 13 is concerned with document set-up, including page size, page orientation and margins.

Chapter 14 is all about printing, including previewing, while in the final chapters we look at some more advanced features of Word 97. Chapter 15 is about how to create, edit and format tables. Chapter 16 is concerned with how to handle pictures, images and drawn objects. In Chapter 17 we shall see how to import objects, such as spreadsheets, into your Word file. Finally, Chapter 18 shows you how to use the Mail Merge features of Word 97.

The guide ends with an index.

Summary

In this chapter:

- We have seen what word processing is.
- We have seen what formatting is.
- We have looked briefly at other word processors.
- We have looked at an outline of the remainder of the book.

★ ECDL ★

First Steps With Word Processing

In this chapter you will learn how to

- *Open and close Word 97.*
- *Open an existing document.*
- *Open more than one document at the same time.*
- *Create a new document.*
- *Save a document onto different media.*
- *Close a document.*
- *Use Word 97 Help functions.*

2.1. Introduction

This chapter is rather long, so you may find it easier to consider it in three sessions, the first concerned with starting Word 97 and finding out about the Word 97 window. In the second session, you can look at opening, saving and closing files, while in the third session you will experiment with Help.

2.2. Opening Word 97

There is no one way to open Word 97. Indeed, there are almost too many ways. Perhaps the two simplest are either to double-click the Word 97 shortcut icon on your desktop (see Figure 2.1) or to click the short-cut icon in the Microsoft Office Shortcut Bar that is created if you install Word as part of the office suite (see Figure 2.2). There are many other ways (see the Information boxes) and you will almost certainly develop your own preferred method, if you have not already done so.

Figure 2.1 The Word icon on the desktop.

Figure 2.2 The Microsoft Office Shortcut bar.

From here on in this book, we shall just refer to Word, rather than Word 97, although you will know that this is what is meant.

You can click Start (at the bottom left of your desktop) and then click on Run. You can then browse through the directories until you find the file (Winword.exe). It will probably be in C:\Program Files\Microsoft Office, but not necessarily.

You can open up the directories on your system by double-clicking on My Computer on the desktop and then successively open directories until you find the Word icon (Figure 2.3) or the file name (this depends on how your windows display the files – see Module 2 of the ECDL).

You can carry out a similar operation using Windows Explorer (most easily opened by clicking with your right mouse button on Start, and then selecting Explore (either by clicking with the left mouse button or by just moving your cursor to Explore; this depends again whether you are using the Classic view or the Web view of your system as discussed in Module 2). You then go down through the directory structure in the same way as for the two approaches above.

For obvious reasons none of these three approaches represents a good way to start an application that you use frequently, although there may be times when any one is appropriate. If for any reason you do not have an obvious icon available on your desktop or the Office toolbar, then the following is the best approach. Click on Start and then move your cursor up to Programs, when the programs stored on your system will be shown on the right. Move the cursor to Microsoft Word and open it (by clicking or double clicking – again this depends on the view you are using). See Figure 2.4. Note, however, that if you are working on a networked system, you are best to check with your system administrator if you have not already been told the recommended way to start Word.

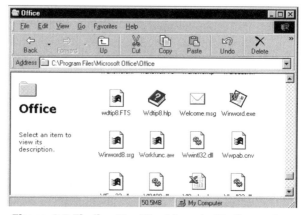

Figure 2.3 Finding the Word icon in My Computer.

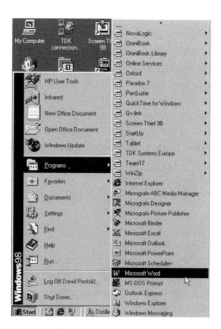

Figure 2.4 Opening Word by following the Start | Programs route.

When you start Word, certainly for the first time and maybe every time, Office Assistant will open (see Figure 2.5). At this stage, click on the **Close** box in the top right corner to close it. We will come back to it in Section 2.9.

★ ECDL ★

Figure 2.5 The Office Assistant.

2.3. The Word Window

Now Word is open and the screen looks like Figure 2.6, where you can see that it is divided into various areas. Now, you may feel that this looks more like an aircraft cockpit than the dashboard of a car, so a pilot's licence, rather than a driving licence would seem to be appropriate. However, you will generally only use one of the commands at a time (each icon represents a command); some of them you will use a lot, while others you may hardly ever use. Different people use Word in different ways and that is why you can customise your Word window, as we shall see in various chapters, although, strictly speaking, this is outside the ECDL syllabus.

Figure 2.6 The opening screen in Word.

Before we go on to describe the different areas of the screen, notice that, when Word starts up, it opens a new document, called **Document1**, and the name is given at the top of the window after the Word icon and, just to remind you, the words 'Microsoft Word'. At the top right of the screen are three icons, common to all Windows applications and described in Module 2.

Exercise 2.3a

If your Word window does not fill the screen, click on the centre icon to maximise the window so that it fills the screen. You will see that there is still the taskbar at the bottom of the screen, which shows the Start button, the applications you have open (Word will be highlighted) and, at the bottom right, various icons representing background tasks in what is called the system tray. To switch between windows and applications you just click on the appropriate place on this bar.

In case you have not read the Module 2 guide, the three icons in the top right of (almost) every Windows application do the following:

Minimise: if you click on this, the title of the application will appear in the bar at the bottom of the screen, but there will be no window open.

Maximise or reduce in size: if the window does not occupy the full screen, then you will see a button which enables you to make it do so, or 'maximise' it. If the window is already occupying the full screen, then you will see a button which reduces the window size.

Close: if you click on this, you will close (exit from) the application. If you click this in Word, depending on what you are doing, you may see a message on the screen, asking, for example, if you want to save the file you have been working on.

shortcut

● **You can close any application by holding down the Alt key and pressing function key F4 (Alt+F4).**
● **You can switch between applications by holding down the Alt key and pressing the Tab key (Alt+Tab). This shows the open windows (see Figure 2.7) with the active window surrounded by a square. If you keep Alt held down and press Tab again, you will see the square move to the next application. You can cycle through all the open windows. To make a window active, you simply release the keys when it is surrounded by the square. It is useful to note that, although you cycle through the operations, when you key Alt+Tab a second time, the previously active window will be active again. This can be very useful if you are switching backwards and forwards between two applications or windows.**

★ ECDL ★

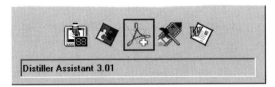

Figure 2.7 Showing the open windows using Alt+Tab.

The second line of the screen applies to the file you have open. On the right there is a Word file icon (a page with the Word icon superimposed – see Figure 2.7).

Exercise 2.3b

● Click on the Word file icon and you will see various commands that allow you to change the document window (which up to now is integrated with the Word window itself).

● Click **Restore** and the document window will become separate (and the Word file icon will move to that window) (Figure 2.8).

● Click **Move** or **Size** and the cursor will change shape and allow you to move either the window as a whole, by clicking in the title bar and moving the cursor and the window (known as drag and drop) or one of its edges.

● Click **Maximize** or **Minimize**. These have the same effect as the symbols at the top right of the window, which you will note are given separately for the document window, so that you can modify or close the document window without having the same effect on the Word window. Note that, if you click **Maximize**, the document window again becomes integrated with the Word window.

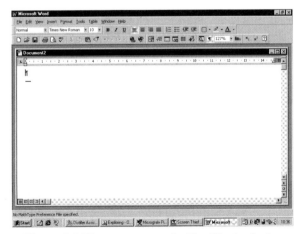

**Figure 2.8 You can separate the Word window
from the document window.**

definition

Drag and drop: Drag and drop means that you place the cursor on what you want to move and depress the left mouse button. Keeping the button depressed, you move the cursor, dragging the icon with it, to the new position. Then you let go of the mouse button and what you were moving (a window, an icon, a file) will stay in the new position, if it is allowed in that position; you may also get a message giving you various options; see Module 2. You can also use drag and drop to move text, as we shall see later.

In most cases you will not use Document1, but you can do so, typing in the text area and saving the document as we shall see in Section 2.7.

On the second line of the screen, there is also a list of words: **File**, **Edit** etc. These are menus and, if you click on them, the menu will drop down; for example, see Figure 2.9. Click again (or elsewhere in the window) and the menu will close. Anything you can do with Word can be accessed from these menus and we shall be looking at many aspects of them as we go through the book. You will notice that in each of the menu names, there is nearly always a letter underlined. What this denotes is a keyboard shortcut, so that keying this letter while holding down the Alt key has the same effect as selecting the menu. Within the menus, you will see that each command also has an underlined letter within it. To select that command, you can just key that letter (do not use the Alt key) as long as the menu is showing.

Figure 2.9 The File drop down menu.

information

In a way Word predates the Web view incorporated in Windows 98. If you put your cursor on a menu name (or any icon), it will be surrounded by a box and to open it, you click once. Similarly, once you have a menu open, as you move the cursor down it, the entries will appear in reverse video (white on blue by default, although it depends on how your system is set up). To select that option you only need to click, rather than double click. Note that the text also gives other approaches.

Below the menu names are one or more toolbars. Note that the toolbars on your system may not be exactly the same as shown in the figure; the Standard and Formatting toolbars are shown by default (Figures 2.10a and 2.10b).

We will look at toolbars in more detail in Chapter 3, but it is worth repeating here that the toolbars contain icons that are graphical equivalents of the commands on the menus.

There are also a few icons at the bottom left of the screen (see Figure 2.6). Clicking the icon is often quicker than accessing the menu and, if you move your cursor over an icon (called mousing over it), the meaning of the icon will be displayed in a small box.

As well as the icons, most commands also have a keyboard equivalent, which is even quicker than clicking an icon. However, you have to remember what the keyboard command is, so you will probably use keyboard commands for operations that you carry out frequently, toolbar icons for common operations that you do not need all the time and menus for less common operations. We shall see examples as we go along and you will develop your own preferred way of accessing different commands.

Figure 2.10a The Standard toolbar in the default state.

Figure 2.10b The Formatting toolbar in the default state.

information

> **Toolbars do not have to be at the top of the screen; they can also be moved around the screen so that they float. If you want to use them in that way, you can, although most people leave them fixed at the top of the screen; in that way, an icon is always in the same place. Sometimes, however, it is useful to display a specific toolbar for a particular task, e.g. editing pictures – and sometimes they even open automatically. In such cases, a floating toolbar can be helpful, because it isolates the operations of current interest. It is also an option to have, say, the Drawing toolbar along the bottom of the document window.**

Below the toolbars, immediately above the text window (as shown in Figure 2.6), is the Ruler, which shows the margins you are using, as discussed in Chapter 13 and any tabs you have set for the line in the text on which the cursor is currently placed. At the left there is a box showing the type of tab you can currently set. See Chapter 9 for more on tabs. If you are in Page Layout view (see Chapter 3), there will also be a ruler down the left-hand side of the page.

On the right hand side of the text window is the vertical scroll bar, which you use to move through the document. You can use this in several ways.

Exercise 2.3c
● In Document 1, depress the Enter (Return) key (add some text if you wish) until you see the sliding box in the scroll bar start to move down.
● Put the cursor on the sliding box and hold down the left mouse button. Then just move the mouse, and thus the box, up or down until you reach the line you want in the text.
● Move the sliding box by pointing at either the single arrow at the top, to move up, or the single arrow at the bottom, to move down the document, and hold the left mouse button down until, again, you reach the line you want.
● Click in the space above or below the sliding box and you will move up or down the document by one screenful; repeat until you see the line you want.

If you have a third button or a wheel on your mouse, you can also use one of these to control scrolling, but this is outside the ECDL syllabus.

Above the top scrolling arrow is a small horizontal bar, which can be used to split the screen, but this is outside the scope of the ECDL syllabus and therefore of this book. We mention it for completeness.

Below the bottom single arrow, you will see two double arrows, with a circle between them. If you mouse over either of the arrows, you will open a box telling you what will happen if you click the double arrow. By default, you go to the next page. Mouse over the circle and it will say **Select Browse Object**. Clicking on the circle will open a menu containing ten icons (see Figure 2.11), from which you can select what you want to happen when you click on the double arrow. If you mouse over an icon, it will be highlighted and in a box below the icons, you will see what the option means.

Some of these you may not understand at this stage, but we will come back to them (although not all), as we go through the book. Note that if you are using Find (Chapter 7), the Browse Object will automatically be set to what you are looking for (this can be disconcerting if you are expecting to go to the next page).

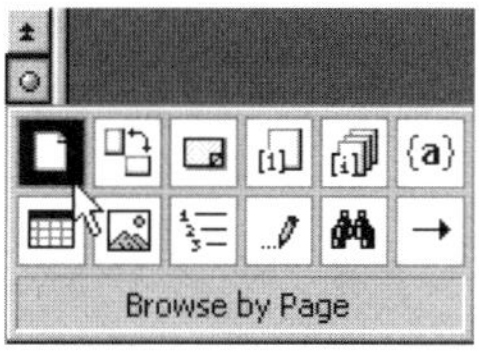

Figure 2.11 Selecting the action for the double arrow buttons.

We have already noted that there is a small toolbar at the bottom left of the screen, containing the view options (see Chapter 3) and alongside this is the horizontal scroll bar, which you can use if your text is wider than the screen. You can use this to move horizontally in exactly the same ways as described above for the vertical scroll bar.

Unless your document is very wide, we suggest that you change the Magnification (see Chapter 3), so that your text fits in the screen window. Although the horizontal cursor will move automatically if you are inputting, this can be very irritating. This is even more the case if you are editing or reading the text, because you have to scroll left and right on every line.

Finally, within the Word window, you have a line that gives you information, known as the Status Bar. From left to right, you see:

● The page number (e.g. Page 4);

● The section number (e.g. Sec 1) – note that sections are outside the ECDL syllabus;

● The page number and the total number of pages (e.g. 4/16);

● The cursor position on the page (e.g. At 17cm) – the unit will depend on what units you have chosen under menu Tools/Options/General;

● The line number where your cursor is placed on the current page (e.g. Ln 25);

● The column number where your cursor is placed on the current line (e.g. Col 79) – in fact, this is not really the column number, but the number of characters to the left of the cursor minus one, so that when you go to a new line this number goes to 1 (before you type anything new); the terminology is really a hangover from the days when all characters were the same width (see Chapter 8 when we discuss fonts);

● Five boxes labelled REC, RTK, EXT, OVR and WPH, describing the current operating mode(s); as you will see as you mouse over them, these stand for Record Macro, Track Changes, Extend Selection, Overtype and WordPerfect Help; within ECDL you only need to be concerned with OVR, which will become darker if you hit the [Ins] (insert) key on your keyboard and will go grey again if you hit [Ins] again – this is called toggling; by default you are in the insert mode, so that if you type something anywhere except at the end of a paragraph, the text moves to the right to make room for the new material. In Overstrike mode, when you type, you overwrite the characters that are already there.

● Then there are two final boxes. The first has an open book in it , which shows the Grammar and Spelling status. See Chapter 12. The last box shows an icon of a diskette when Word is saving your file in the background. This is a security measure, so that if your system crashes you can get back your work up to the last background save, even if you haven't saved what you have done. You can set how often background saves take place by accessing menu **Tools | Options | Save**; you can also turn them off if you wish, but this is not a good idea. It is also a good idea to leave **Always create backup copy** ticked, so that you have the previous version of a file to go back to.

★ ECDL ★

caution!

> **Note that Word will only save a security copy that can be used for recovery after a crash if you have saved the file at least once. If you do not give the file a name, then you will lose your work!**

Note that, even when the Word window is set for full screen, you can still see the system bar at the bottom of the screen. Depending on how your system is set up, there may also be an Office toolbar (or maybe a Windows toolbar) down the right-hand side of the screen.

Self Study

1. Open Word (choose your method) and examine the Word window. Mouse over icons. Open menus. Try typing some text into Document1 if you have not done so already, but do not save. If ever in doubt when you see a screen that requires an answer, click on **Cancel**. (Note that you can do no harm, as long as you do not open an existing document and save it after making any changes.) Once you have finished, close Word by clicking the **Close** box in the top right corner (click on **No** when asked if you want to save changes to Document1).

2. Open Word again (try a different method this time). Type a few sentences. Zoom in to make the text larger (click on the down arrow by the percentage – probably 100% – on the Standard toolbar (see Figure 2.10(a)) and increase to, say, 200%). Now (a) type some more and see what happens to the text in the window and (b) try to read the text you have typed, using the horizontal scroll bar to take you back and forth across the page width.

2.4. Opening an Existing Document

Exercise 2.4a

To open an existing document, click on the **File** menu and then on **Open...** (**File | Open**... – from here on we will omit the stops after the command name). You will then see a window that looks like Figure 2.12. This contains a large number of ways to specify a file, but at present we will only look at some of the options. First, since we are going to open a Word document, we go to the box at the bottom left of the window (**Files of type:**). If it already shows **Word Documents (*.doc)**, then you do not need to change anything. If it says anything else, then, if you click the down arrow on the right of the box, you will see a list of options that you can scroll down. Choose **Word Documents (*.doc)** by clicking on it and only files with the extension .doc (the extension used by Word) will appear in the main file-name window. You can achieve the same thing by typing *.*doc* in the box labelled **File name:** and then keying Enter.

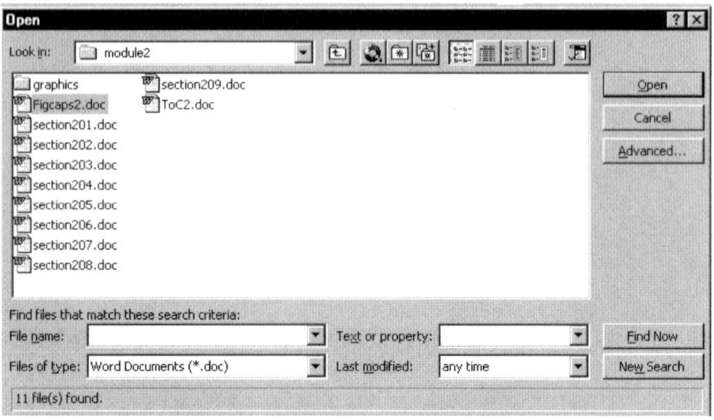

Open

Look in:	module2

graphics
Figcaps2.doc
section201.doc
section202.doc
section203.doc
section204.doc
section205.doc
section206.doc
section207.doc
section208.doc
section209.doc
ToC2.doc

Open
Cancel
Advanced...

Find files that match these search criteria:

File name:		Text or property:		Find Now
Files of type:	Word Documents (*.doc)	Last modified:	any time	New Search

11 file(s) found.

Figure 2.12 Opening an existing document.

Next, you need to see if you are in the directory where the file you want is stored. The first time you open a file in a Word session, you will probably not be (by default you will probably be in **My Documents**), so you need to browse.

Here you use the same technique as is described above for looking for the Word application file. This assumes that you know where the file is that you want to open. More often than not, this will be the case, particularly if you have organised your directory structure in a logical way (see Module 2).

However, if, like all of us, you sometimes cannot remember exactly what the file name was that you gave to a file or where you saved it, the **Open** dialogue box gives various ways that you can find the file. These are outside the scope of the ECDL syllabus, but are fairly easy to understand.

Once you have found the directory you want, you may wish to find out more about the files therein. The icons to the right (see Figure 2.12) allow you to view different aspects of the file. Figures 13a to 13d show these different aspects.

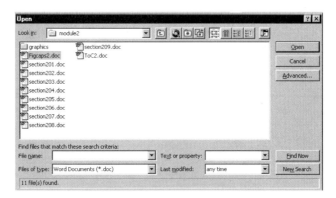

Figure 2.13a A simple list of files.

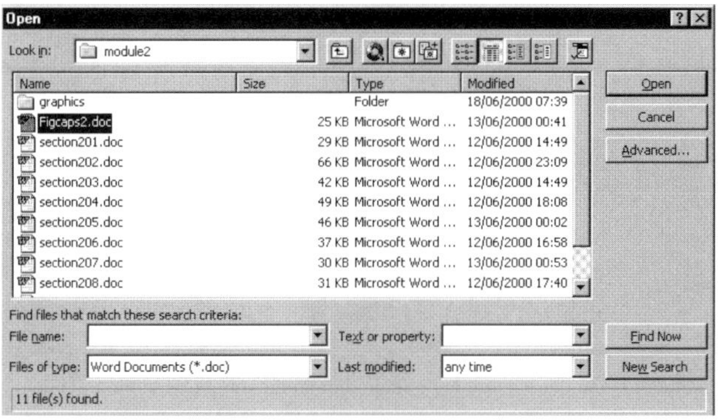

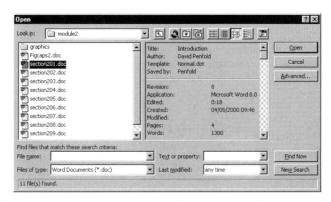

Figure 2.13b More information about the file, such as its size and when it was last modified.

Figure 2.13c Additional information about the individual file.

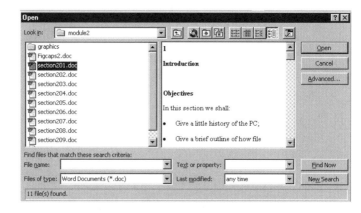

Figure 2.13d A preview of the file.

The last icon, **Commands and settings**, provides you with other options outside the ECDL syllabus.

Exercise 2.4b

Once you have decided which file you want to open, you can either double click on it or you can select it with a single click and then click **Open**. If you know the full name of the file you wish to open, you can enter that in the 'File name:' box and key Enter. Then you will only see one file listed in the main file-name window, so all you need to do is click **Open**.

If you want to open a file that you have worked on recently, then, by clicking on the **File** menu, almost at the bottom (immediately above **Exit**), you will see a list of file names (how many depends on how your system has been set up; the number can be changed by using **Tools | Options | General**, with the maximum number being nine). These are the last files you saved with the most recent first. To open one of these files, just click on the file name. Note that, if they are not in the directory in which the file you are currently working on is stored, then the full path (disk drive name plus directory tree) is given.

shortcut

Instead of clicking on File and then on Open, you can just type Ctrl+O, which will achieve the same thing or you can click the Open file icon on the tool bar.

★ ECDL ★

shortcut

Note that instead of clicking Open in the File Open window, you can just key Enter. This will always be the case when you have a sub-window open, when striking Enter will be the same as clicking on the box that is highlighted. Be careful, however, if you use this approach, which is undoubtedly faster, to ensure that the option you want is indeed highlighted!

2.5. Opening Several Documents

You can open almost as many documents as you like at the same time (the size of the memory on your computer is the main factor limiting the number; along with the number of other applications you have open).

You open each file in the way described above. To move between them, you click the **Window** menu and you will see the files you have open listed at the bottom. Just click on the one that you want to bring it to the front. By using split screen and changing the sizes of the document windows, you can view more than one file at the same time (this is outside the ECDL syllabus).

2.6. Creating a New Document

There are three ways to open a new document:

Exercise 2.6

● Click on the **New document** icon ☐ on the toolbar. This will immediately open a new document in whatever view you are currently using; we will deal with views in Chapter 3.

● Type Ctrl+N. This is the keyboard shortcut for the above and the effect will be the same.

● Go to the **File** menu and select **New**. This will open a window that looks like Figure 2.14. Choose the icon that is labelled **Blank Document**. If your system is new, this may be the only one visible. Make sure that, under **Create New**, **Document** (rather than **Template**) is selected. We will discuss templates in Chapter 10, when we will come back to all the other tabs shown in Figure 2.14.

Open Word and type a letter, putting your address (or whatever address you want to use at the top) and using the usual forms of address. Perhaps you could tell a friend about doing the ECDL course? Do not be concerned with formatting or typefaces etc. Just use the typeface that appears when you type and allow everything to align left.

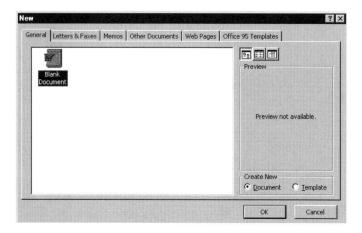

Figure 2.14 Creating a new document via the File menu.

2.7. Saving a Document

There are three ways of saving a document:

Exercise 2.7

● Click on the **Save file** icon ⊞ on the toolbar. If the document is new, then you will see a window like that shown in Figure 2.15. To save as a Word file, all you need to do is make sure that the name suggested is acceptable, changing it if it is not, and ensure that the file will be saved in the correct directory. The window is, in fact, quite similar to the **Open** file window and the icons mean the same. There is one icon ⊡ that we have not seen previously; this allows you to create a new subdirectory within the current directory. Once you have determined the name and place for the file, then click **OK**. You will then see an expanding bar at the bottom left of the Word window, tracking the progress of the save. If you are saving a file that has previously been saved, then you will only see the progress bar and not the **Save** window.

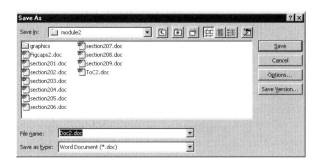

Figure 2.15 Saving a new document.

● Go to the **File** menu and select **Save**. This will have the same effect as clicking the icon.

● Type Ctrl+S. This is the keyboard shortcut and again the effect will be the same.

If you have not already carried out the exercise in Module 2 in which you created a directory (in My Documents) called **ECDL**, with subdirectories for each module, then we suggest you do so now. Start to save your document and you will see the **Save** menu (Figure 2.15). Make sure that you are in the **My Documents** directory and click on the **Create a New Folder** icon. Type in the name *ECDL* and then open that directory by double clicking or single clicking and then clicking **Open**. (If you wish, you can then create a subdirectory called Module 3.) Once you are sure that you are in the directory where you want to save your file, decide what you want to call your file, perhaps *letter01.doc* or *test01.doc* and then click on **Save** (note that when you have a directory selected this button changes to **Open**). We shall come back to this file as we go though the book and we shall refer to it as **test01** (and others as **test02** etc.). Please also save the file as *test02.doc*, perhaps after making a few changes.

2.8. Saving a File Under a New Name, in a Different Directory or on a Different Medium

If, when you are working on a file that has been saved before, instead of selecting Save, you can select **Save As** in the **File** menu. The procedure is the same as if you were saving a new file; you can change the name of the file and/or the directory in which you save it.

You can also save onto a different medium. When you browse through directories, if you keep pressing the **Up One Level** icon, you will eventually reach **My Computer** and you will see the drives on your system listed (see Figure 2.16). Then you select the drive you want (making sure, if appropriate, that there is a formatted disk in the drive) and next move down the directory structure, creating directories if you wish. When you reach the level where you want to save the file, you click the **Save** button.

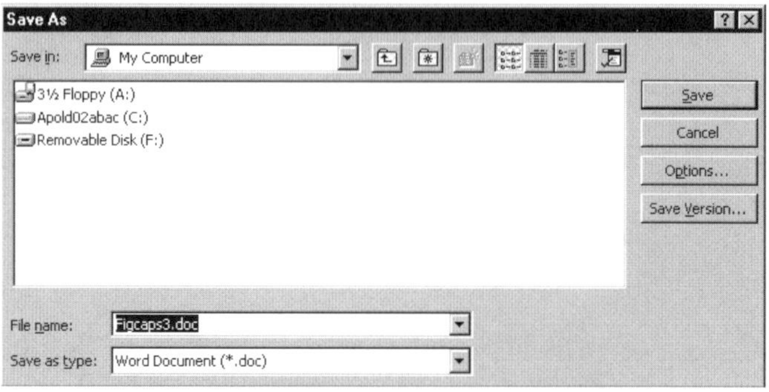

Figure 2.16 Saving on a new medium.

We shall discuss saving in other formats in Chapter 4.

information

> If you want to use a file as a kind of 'unofficial template', for example you are using one letter as the basis for another, it is a good idea to save it under a new file name before you make any changes. If you do not do this and go ahead and make the changes, there is always the chance that you will click on Save and overwrite your original file. While your system may have been set up to keep a backup of the original file, it is much easier if you do not have to use it.

2.9. Closing a Document and Closing Word

Exercise 2.8a

To close a document, you can do one of the following:

● Go to the **File** menu and select **Close** (**File I Close**).
● Click on the Word document icon on the left of File and then on **Close**.

● Click on the **Close** box at the top right-hand corner of the document window (not the one at the top of the screen, which will exit from Word).
● Type Ctrl+W.

If the document you are closing has not been saved, then you will be prompted to save it.

Exercise 2.8b

To close Word, you can do one of the following:

● Go to the **File** menu and select **Exit** (**File I Exit**).
● Click on the Word icon in the title bar and then on **Close**.
● Click on the **Close** box at the top right-hand corner of the screen.
● Type Ctrl+F4 (function key 4).

If there are any open documents that you have not saved, then you will be prompted to save them.

2.10. Using Help

There are various ways you can obtain help on using Word. With earlier versions, you would have received a fairly large printed manual, but today almost all help is provided electronically, which should mean that it is easier to locate what you want to know. Even now, however, there are different approaches you can take.

The first of these is called the Office Assistant, which we already noted will probably appear the very first time you use Word. The rather sly-looking character, based on a paper clip, is called Clippit.

To open Office Assistant, if it is not already open, click on the **Question Mark** icon ⟦?⟧ on the toolbar, press function key F1 or go to the **Help** menu and select **Microsoft Help**. Clippit will then appear, as in Figure 2.17, asking you what you would like to do. If you type in a question and then click **Search**, Clippitt will do its best to answer it. Some options will then appear. If you select one of these, then a relevant Help screen will appear (Figure 2.18).

Once you have read that screen and any others that may be linked to it (and even printing it if you wish by clicking on **Options** and selecting **Print**) you can close it by using the **Close** box at the top right corner. To reactivate the Office Assistant, just click on him (or press function key F1) and you will find the same display as in Figure 2.17. You can then click on a different option.

What would you like to do?

- Change the font of text or numbers

- Change the size of text or numbers

- Set the default font

- Change the color of text and numbers

- Let Word format my documents and WordMail messages

▼ See more...

How do I change a font?

● Search

● Tips   ● Options   ● Close

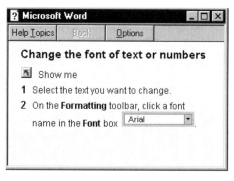

Figure 2.17 The Clippit Office Assistant.

Microsoft Word

| Help Topics | Back | Options |

Change the font of text or numbers

Show me

1 Select the text you want to change.

2 On the **Formatting** toolbar, click a font name in the **Font** box Arial .

Figure 2.18 A Help screen.

If you do not like Clippit, there are a number of other characters that you can use. To access these and other ways of customising Office Assistant, you need to click **Options** in the Office Assistant window. The Gallery tab will allow you to move through the various alternative characters (Figure 2.19), but perhaps more important are the Options themselves. Most of these are fairly self-explanatory. A word, however, about Tips.

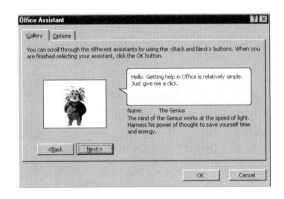

Figure 2.19 The Office Assistant Gallery, showing an alternative character to Clippit.

Depending which options you have selected, then when Office Assistant 'thinks' that you could do what you are doing more efficiently, a light bulb will appear in the top right corner of the Office Assistant window. If you click on that, you will see the tip (see Figures 2.20a and 2.20b).

Figure 2.20a The Office Assistant displays a light bulb to show it has a tip for you.

Figure 2.20b The tip itself.

If you no longer find Office Assistant helpful, you can close it. You should also note that, when you are using Office Assistant, all messages appear in the Office Assistant message box, rather than in an ordinary dialogue box, so it is possible that you may miss them because Office Assistant has become a fixture that you tend to ignore.

You can also use Help in a more conventional way. Go the Help menu, at which point you have two choices (in addition to opening Office Assistant):

● Select **What's this?** The **Question Mark** icon 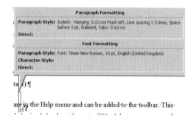 appears in the **Help** menu and can be added to the toolbar. This will provide you with context-sensitive help, i.e. help about the part of Word that you are currently using. Your cursor will change to the icon and when you click in any part of the Word window a small window will open giving you information (see Figure 2.21). To cancel this click again on either the toolbar icon or the menu option.

Figure 2.21 A Help window produced by selecting What's This?

● Click on **Contents and Index**.

As you can see from Figure 2.22, Help is self-explanatory, as indeed it should be if it is going to be much use. A little explanation may be helpful, however, specifically for **Contents**, **Index** and **Find**:

● **Contents** gives you the view shown in Figure 2.22. If you are learning about the system or are not really sure, this is probably the easiest approach.

Figure 2.22 The Help screen showing Contents.

★ ECDL ★

● Index gives you a 'back-of-the-book' type index (see Figure 2.23) and this is quick if you know what you are looking for and if you know the term Microsoft uses, which may not always be obvious!

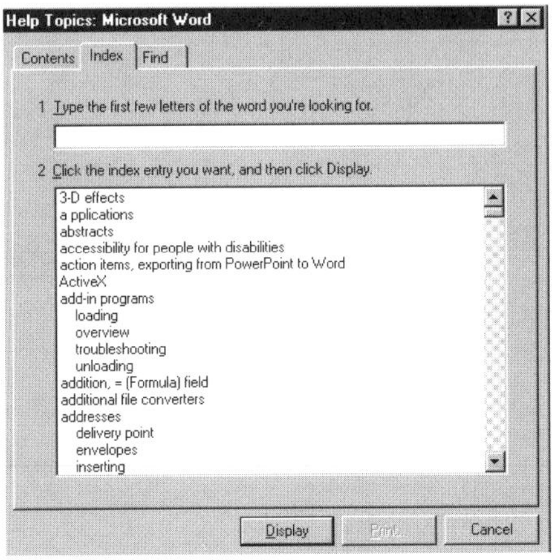

Figure 2.23 The Help screen showing Index.

● Find (see Figure 2.24) allows you to search for any word. You put in the word or phrase and then follow the instructions. This will eventually yield what you want if it is there.

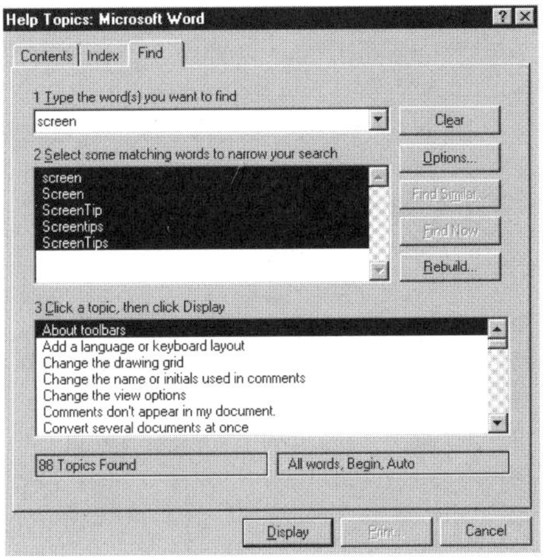

Figure 2.24 The Help screen showing Find.

The final option in the **Help** menu is **About Microsoft Word** and this will give you information on various aspects of the program (Figure

2.25) and indeed your system, if you click **System Info**. Note that there is also a **Technical Support** button that opens special Help screens that tell you about Microsoft Technical Support.

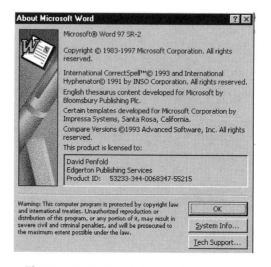

**Figure 2.25 The result of selecting the
About Microsoft Word option.**

Self Study

Experiment with the different ways that you can find help. Don't worry about finding information about a specific topic (although you may want to do that), but ensure that you are happy about the ways in which help can be obtained so that you can decide which approach you prefer.

Summary

In this chapter:

● We have seen how to open Word.
● We have examined the Word window.
● We have seen how to open one or more existing documents.
● We have seen how to create a new document.
● We have seen how to save a document.
● We have seen how to save a document under a new name, in a new directory or on a different medium.
● We have seen how to close a document and how to close Word.
● We have seen ways of using Help.

Adjusting Basic Settings

In this chapter you will learn how to

- *Change the basic settings.*
- *Change the page magnification.*
- *Modify the toolbar display.*

3.1. Introduction

One of the great advantages of Word (and many other modern programs) is that, in many ways, you can choose to use them as you want to, rather than as the software designer felt was the right way. There are, of course, always things that you would like to change but cannot. Here we shall look at some of those you can.

3.2. Changing Display Modes

If you look at the **View** menu, you will see that there are five display modes listed:

● **Normal**, which is probably the easiest to work with, in that the text fills the Word window (Figure 3.1) and page breaks are just indicated by a broken line across the screen. It is important to remember, however, that neither drawings and artwork in boxes nor page headers and footers appear in this view, so you need to be careful if you have these things in your document.

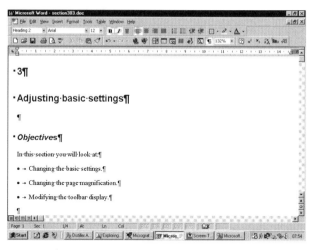

Figure 3.1 Normal view.

● **Online Layout**, which splits the window into two panes, with a table of contents in the left-hand pane (Figure 3.2). It is fairly important that you use styles to take advantage of this view (see Chapter 10). Its big advantage is that if you click on one of the headings in the left pane, you will jump to the appropriate place in the document.

★ ★ ★
★ ECDL ★
★ ★ ★

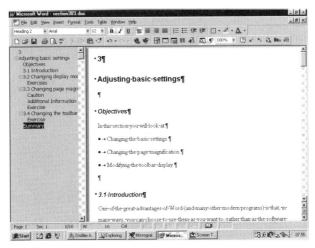

Figure 3.2 Online Layout view.

● **Page Layout**, which shows you how your document will appear when printed, with all the graphics etc. (Figure 3.3).

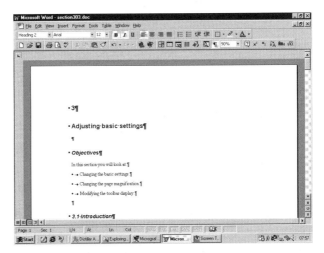

Figure 3.3 Page Layout view.

● **Outline**, which allows you to see the structure of your document, again using the heading styles (Figure 3.4).

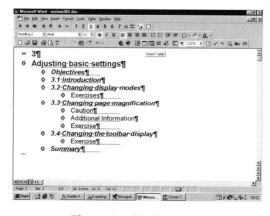

Figure 3.4 Outline view.

● **Master Document**, which is used when you group a number of documents into a larger one. This is outside the scope of ECDL and is, in any case, not always predictable.

These views can also be accessed from the tool bar at the bottom left of the window (see Figure 3.5).

Figure 3.5 The View toolbar.

Self Study

1. Open **test01.doc** or **test02.doc**. Experiment with the **Normal** and **Page Layout** views. The latter will give you a good idea, for example, if your letter will fit on a single page.

2. If you have access to a longer Word file, including headings etc., open it and experiment with the **Online Layout** and **Outline views**.

3.3. Changing Page Magnification

You can change the page size of a document, as well as the type sizes within it, as we shall see in Chapter 8. However, it is convenient to be able to see the text at a larger size, so as to make editing easier (although that may lead to problems, as noted in Chapter 2, if the page width is wider than the screen). You may also wish to see a number of pages at a smaller size so as to obtain an overall impression of the layout. Remember, however, that in either case, you are changing how you look at the document and not the document itself.

★ ECDL ★

Exercise 3.3

You can set the page magnification in two ways:

● Go to the toolbar, where you will see the box (Figure 3.6a) that allows you to pick/specify the view size as a percentage; the current percentage will already be shown. If you click the **down arrow** on the right-hand side, you see a list of fixed percentages, plus **Page Width**. Just click on one of these and the magnification will change. Alternatively, you can type the percentage you want to use directly in the box and then press the Enter key. If you choose **Page Width**, the system will calculate the percentage so that your text (in Normal view) or the page (in Page Layout view) will fill the width of the page.

Figure 3.6a Zoom options on the toolbar.

● Go to the **View** menu and select **Zoom**. You will now see a window (Figure 3.6b) with a selection of percentages, as well as **Page Width** and, if you're using Page Layout, **Whole Page** and **Many Pages**. Your present percentage is shown bottom left and you can again type directly into this box or pick from the list. Whole Page, of course, shows the whole page on the screen, while, if you choose **Many Pages**, you can click on the computer icon to choose from a series of preset layouts (Figure 3.6c). You can also see a preview. Click **OK** when you are happy with what you have.

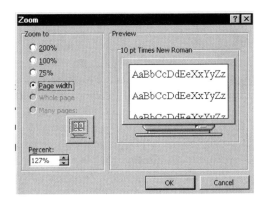

Figure 3.6b The zoom options obtained from View I Zoom.

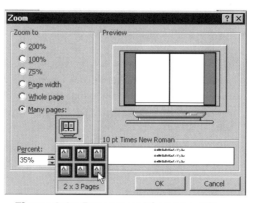

Figure 3.6c Pre-set multi-page options.

caution!

Although you are specifying percentages, it is not really very clear exactly what they are percentages of. If you choose 100%, then the type size on screen is not the same as it would be on paper. It will partly depend on the size of your screen. Thus it is unwise to use what you see on the screen as a final guide to type sizes in the final printed document. Although zooming is referred to, this is not a graphical zoom like those in many graphics programs, where the area of interest is selected and zooming changes the view so that the area of interest fills the screen window. Note that the Page Width magnification in the Online layout does not have any real meaning. This is because the text in the right-hand pane 'wraps'. This means that the line length is adjusted to fill the width of the window.

information

Each layout view retains its own magnification, so that, if you change the magnification in Normal, you do not alter it in, for example, Page Layout.

Self Study

Continue with the files you had open in the earlier examples in this chapter and change the magnification in the different views to see what the effects are and whether larger sizes are helpful or present a problem.

3.4. Changing the Toolbar Display

The toolbars, as described in Chapter 2, are sets of icons that represent tools (or operations that you can carry out). Word comes with a number of toolbars already prepared. To see a list, go to the **View** menu and select **Toolbars** (see Figure 3.7). To see what is on each toolbar, if you can select one, it will appear at the top of the screen (those that are ticked are already showing). To remove a toolbar, just open the **Toolbars** window again and deselect it. It is obviously impractical to have all the toolbars on the screen, so you need to choose which ones are most useful to you. Indeed, depending on what you are doing, you may change your selection from task to task.

Figure 3.7 List of available toolbars.

As noted earlier, with a few exceptions, such as the Layout toolbar in the bottom left of the Word window, most toolbars can be moved around the screen. If a toolbar is 'locked' at the top of the window, then place the cursor on the double lines at the left and just 'drag and drop' (Figure 3.8a). If the toolbar is floating, you place the cursor in the title bar at the top of the toolbar window (Figure 3.8b). Note that when the toolbar is floating, you see what it is called, which is not the case when it is 'locked' at the top of the window. As noted in Chapter 2, you may find it helpful to use floating toolbars when you are carrying out a specific task.

Figure 3.8a A fixed toolbar.

Figure 3.8b Moving a floating toolbar by dragging its title bar.

You may have noticed that at the bottom of the Toolbars window it says **Customize**. This is outside the ECDL syllabus, but it is worth experimenting with once you are more confident, because you may want to add to the toolbars icons that are appropriate to the work you do. You can even create your own if you wish!

The icons on the toolbars are not really self-explanatory, except perhaps in a few cases. However, to find out what they mean, just move your cursor over (mouse over) the icon and a small box will appear telling you what it means. There is a certain knack in doing this, so move the cursor around over the icon if the box does not appear immediately. You will get to know the icons you use regularly.

Self Study

Look at the list of toolbars in the **View** menu. Select as many as you can and mouse over the icons, so as to try and familiarise yourself with what they mean. Try moving the toolbars so that they are fixed and floating.

Summary

In this chapter we have seen how to:

● Change display modes (or views).
● Change the page magnification.
● Change the toolbar display.

Saving Documents in Other Formats

In this chapter you will learn how to

- *Save a document as a simple text file.*

- *Save a document for use in other versions of Word and other word processors.*

- *Save a document in Rich Text Format (RTF).*

- *Save as a document template.*

- *Save different versions of a document.*

- *Save a document in a form that can be put up on the World Wide Web.*

4.1. Introduction

You may not always want your document as a Word document, for example you may want a web version, or you may want to send it to someone who has an earlier version of Word or someone who is using, for example, WordPerfect or Word on a Macintosh. Thus Word provides ways of saving documents in other formats.

4.2. Saving a Document as a Simple Text File

As discussed in Chapter 1, while Word documents include formatting information when they are saved, so that next time you open them they have the same appearance as previously, there are times when you only want to save the text, i.e. the letters and spaces, plus punctuation, carriage returns and tab characters. These are known as simple text files (usually with the file extension .txt, although others are used as well).

Exercise 4.2a

To save a file in text format, go to the **File** menu and select **Save As**, just as you did in Chapter 2 when you wanted to save a document under a different name. This time, however, as well as selecting the file name and the directory where you want to save it, go the drop-down menu **Save as type** (Figure 4.1). Here you will see a list of various options, which you can scroll down. Near the top, however, you will see various **.txt** options:

- Text only.
- Text only with line breaks.
- MS-DOS text.

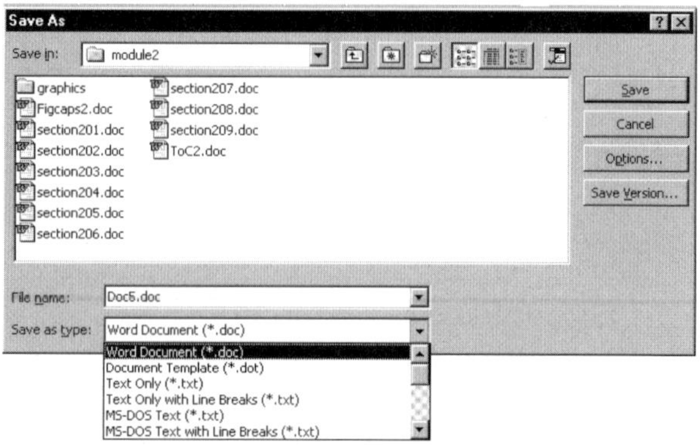

Figure 4.1 Save as type: box expanded.

- MS-DOS text with line breaks.
- Unicode with line breaks.

The last three you can ignore for the purposes of ECDL; they code accented characters and other symbols in different ways from Windows. The difference between the first two is simple. **Text only** includes a carriage return only at the end of each paragraph, whereas **Text only with line breaks** adds a carriage return at the end of each line, as it appears in the Word document. The latter may be useful if you are going to use the text file in some application where the text is not automatically 'wrapped' (although such applications are less common today than they used to be). Note that, if you do not include it, Word will add the .txt file extension.

Although when you save as text, the existing formatting remains on the screen, if you close the file and reopen it in Word, you will find that all the formatting you added has disappeared. The other thing to note (and this applies to all saves in different formats) is that the file name and the file extension in the title bar will have changed. Thus you are now looking at the new file and not the Word file. If you want to go back to working on the Word file, you need to reopen it. You should remember that if you want subsequent changes saved in the new format you will have to use **Save As** again. You will then see a message asking you if you wish to overwrite the previous file or not. Click **OK** to accept.

Exercise 4.2b

Open **test01.doc**. Although it has very little formatting, it will almost certainly be in a typeface such as Times. Save it as *test01.txt* and (with line breaks) as *test03.txt*. Close the file(s) and then reopen them and notice the differences.

4.3. Saving a Document for Use in Other Versions of Word and Other Word Processors

Word makes it extremely easy to save a document for use with earlier versions of Word, or indeed other word processors.

Exercise 4.3

Click on **Save As** in the **File** menu and look through the **Save as type** list until you see what you want. This list contains various versions of WordPerfect and Word 6.0/95 (as well as RTF and HTML, which we shall consider in the following sections); see Figure 4.2.

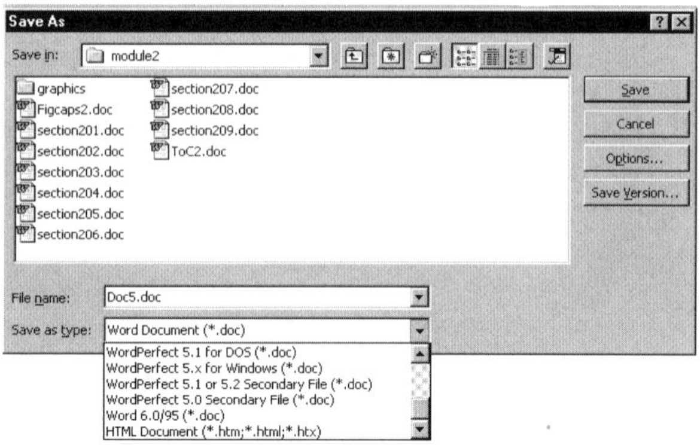

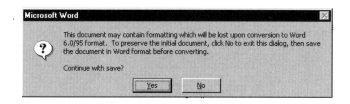

Figure 4.2 Different view of the Save as type: box.

You simply choose the option you want, as for text files, and **Save**. Again the correct file extension will be added if you do not include it. Note that if you save in **Word 6.0/95**, you will see a warning that you may lose some of the formatting (Figure 4.3).

Figure 4.3 Warning window displayed if you save a Word file as as an earlier version of Word.

4.4. Saving a Document for Use in Rich Text Format

Rich Text Format (RTF) was invented by Microsoft as a document interchange language for moving documents between word processors and, indeed, most word processing programs, and some other programs, can now open files saved as RTF, which can be useful. As noted earlier, an RTF file is actually a text file with all the formatting instructions spelt out as codes. Part of the file of this section as originally entered looks as follows in RTF:

★ ECDL ★

{\b 4

\par }\pard \sb60\sl360\slmult1\widctlpar\outlinelevel0\adjustright {\b Saving documents in other formats

\par }\pard \sb60\sl360\slmult1\widctlpar\adjustright {\b

\par }\pard \sb60\sl360\slmult1\widctlpar\outlinelevel0\adjustright {\b Objectives

\par }\pard \sb60\sl360\slmult1\widctlpar\adjustright {In this section you will learn how to:

\par {\pntext\pard\plain\f3\fs20\cgrid \loch\af3\dbch\af0\hich\f3 \'b7\tab}}\pard \fi-360\li360\sb60\sl360\slmult1\widctlpar\jclisttab\tx360{*\pn \pnlvlblt\ilvl0\ls12\pnrnot0\pnf3\pnstart1\pnindent360\pnhang{\pntxtb \'b7}}\ls12\adjustright {

Save a document as a simple text file

Before this passage, which is the start of the text, there is a very long section, often called the preamble, which specifies almost all aspects of the layout. This is often longer than the file itself!

As you can see, RTF is not a reader-friendly language, but it does not need to be as it only really needs to be understood by other word processing programs. If you open an RTF file in Word, you may be asked to confirm that it is RTF or it may just open like a Word file; this depends on how your system is set up, but normally you will never see coding like that above, unless you want to.

To save in this format, again use **Save As** and this time select **Rich Text Format**. Word will automatically change the extension to .rtf.

information

Word can be set up to ask for confirmation when a file is opened in a format that is not Word. In the Tools menu, select Options and then the General tab. You will see that one of the entries is Confirm conversion at Open. If this is ticked, then you will be asked to confirm that a file is indeed RTF, for example. You can simply click Open or you can select Text only instead and then click Open. You will then see the RTF as text. The same can be done for HTML files. If you do this with other file types, you simply see a screen of characters that will make no sense to you. Note that if you try to open a file in an incorrect format, other than as a text file, then Word will tell you that this is not possible.

Exercise 4.4

Open your file **text01.doc** and save it as **RTF**. Close it and then reopen it. Did it open immediately or ask you to confirm? If the latter, key **Open**. In either case you should find that the file appears identical with the original Word file. If you want to see the RTF file, ensure that **Confirm on Open** is selected and then select **text** in this box, as discussed. As your file is quite short, go to the end of the file and work up until you find the start of your file. Looking at the position of the box on the vertical scroll bar will give you an idea of what proportion of the file the preamble takes up.

4.5. Saving a Document as a Template

We shall look at document templates in Chapter 10, but all you need to know now is that a template stores all the formatting information that you have created. It can contain text, but does not have to. When you create a new document using **File | New**, you have a choice of templates, as we shall see in Chapter 10.

Exercise 4.5

If you want to save a file as a template, you can delete all the text that is specific to the document, but leave, for example, your address in a letter template and then go to **Save As** and choose **Document Template** in the **Save as type** box. You will notice two things (Figure 4.4):

● The file extension changes from **.doc** to **.dot**. You may also want to change the file name to something that is more generic and describes the template type rather than this particular file.
● The directory changes to one called **Templates**. Until you have more experience, it is wise to accept this and store the new template in this directory. In this way, when you open a new document with **File | New**, your new template will be one of the choices offered to you.

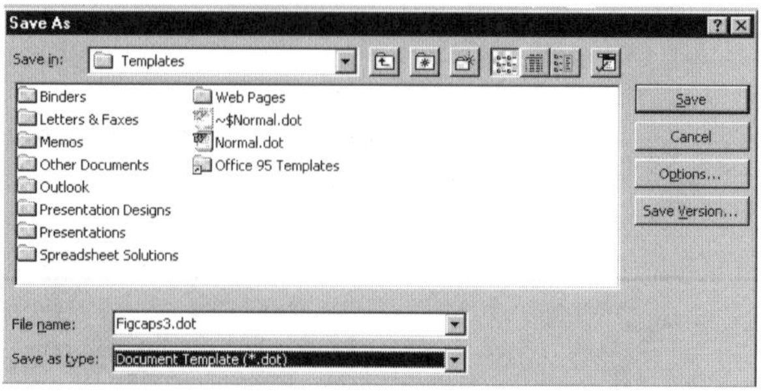

Figure 4.4 Saving a file as a template.

Self Study

While you can open **text01.doc** and look at saving it as a template, we recommend that you only look and do not save. The file as yet contains too little formatting information to make saving it as a template worth while.

4.6. Saving Versions of a Document

There may be situations where you want to save different versions of a document without changing the file name.

Exercise 4.6a

If you choose **Save As** and click **Save Version**, you can save different versions of a document all in the same file. You have the opportunity to add comments to each version (Figure 4.5a) and when you reopen the file, you will see the latest version. If you go to the **File** menu and select **Versions**, a window like Figure 4.5b will appear. You can open earlier versions by selecting them and clicking **Open**. You can also delete previous versions and so on.

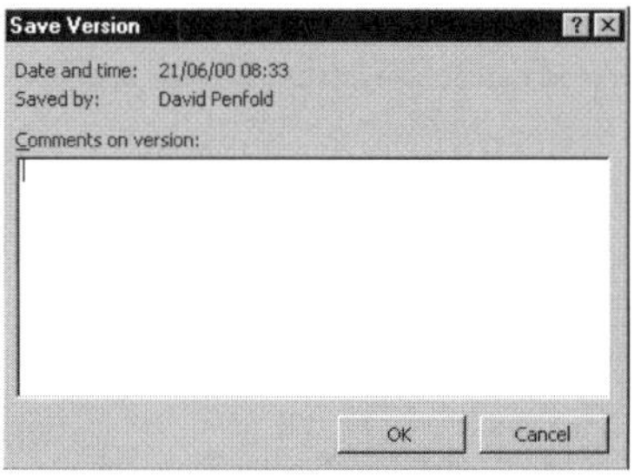

Figure 4.5a The option to add comments.

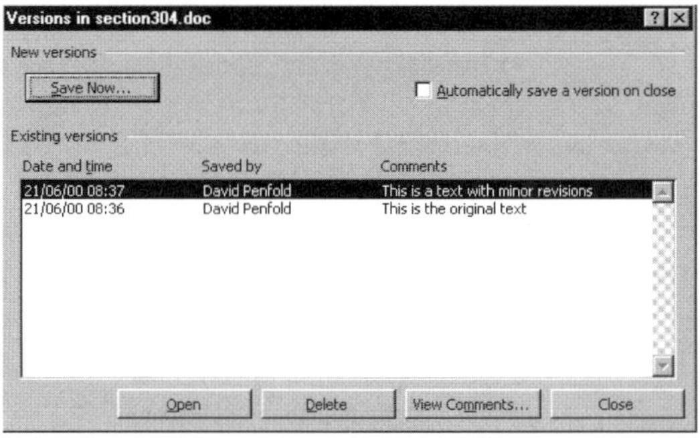

Figure 4.5b The opportunity to review earlier versions.

Exercise 4.6b

Open **text01.doc**. Make a few changes and then save the new version. Make a few more and save another version. Review your versions. When you have finished, delete all except the original and the most recent version.

4.7. Saving a Document in a Form That Can Be Put Up on the World Wide Web

The World Wide Web uses a coding system called HyperText Markup Language (HTML) with which to describe formatting. A web browser, such as Internet Explorer or Netscape Navigator, interprets this language in just the same way as Word interprets RTF, so that you do not see the coding on the screen. HTML carries out a similar task to RTF and is also a text file, but it is much simpler. The same text as we saw above looks like the following in HTML:

```
<HTML>
<HEAD>
<META HTTP-EQUIV="Content-Type" CONTENT="text/html; charset=windows-1252">
<META NAME="Generator" CONTENT="Microsoft Word 97">
<TITLE>2 First steps with word processing </TITLE>
</HEAD>
<BODY>

<B><FONT SIZE=2><P>4</P>
<P>Saving documents in other formats</P>
<P> </P>
<P>Objectives</P>
</B><P>In this section you will learn how to:</P>

<UL>
<LI>Save a document as a simple text file</LI>
```

This is the beginning of the file and there is no preamble like that in RTF. This is partly because much of the formatting information is stored in the web browser, although you can open HTML documents in Word and save them as Word files. Again, however, you do not ever need to see this coding.

Exercise 4.7a

To save as HTML, you can either use **Save As** as before and choose **HTML document** or you can choose **Save as HTML** directly from the **File** menu.

When you save as HTML, you will find that the screen layout changes to look more like a web browser. This is a version of the Online layout, but with only one window and this is built into the template, which changes when you open an HTML file. You can switch to other layouts in just the same way as for an ordinary Word file.

Exercise 4.7b

Open **text01.doc** and save it as an HTML document. See what happens to the screen. If you have a web browser available (see Module 7 for more information on this topic), you can try opening the html file, which will now have an extension .htm, to see what it looks like. Since it has very little formatting, it will probably look very uninteresting.

caution!

It is possible to set up Word without the facility to save as HTML, so if you do not see this option, speak to your systems manager, your supplier or even the Microsoft Helpline. Alternatively, someone with experience may be able to help you reinstall Word or install the extra module.

Summary

In this chapter:

- We have looked at saving a document as a text file.
- We have looked at saving a document for use in other versions of Word and other word processors.
- We have looked at saving a document as an RTF file.
- We have looked at saving a document as a template.
- We have looked at saving the file as an HTML file for use on the Web.

Inserting, Deleting and Editing Characters

5

In this chapter you will learn how to

- *Insert and delete characters, words, sentences, paragraphs and special characters, such as fixed spaces or mathematical symbols.*

- *Insert a page break.*

- *Use the undo command.*

5.1. Introduction

Most of this chapter is about the basics of word processing, getting text (characters and spaces) onto the page. Of course, if you open a new document, all you need to do initially is type, just as you would on a typewriter. You will have already seen that, when you reach the right-hand margin that has been set up for you, the next word automatically appear on the next line and, when you press the Enter key, you generate a carriage return that starts a new line. Similarly, you can enter tab characters and the cursor will move to a fixed preset position in the line, just as it does with a typewriter.

This is fine as long as you only want to type the characters you can see on the keyboard and if you do not need to change anything. We shall see in later chapters how you can change the appearance and formatting of text, but here we consider how to change the text you have already entered and how to enter characters that are not on the keyboard. We will also see how to undo an edit.

5.2. Editing and Deleting Characters

In Chapter 6 we shall discuss selecting and deleting more than one character at a time. However if you want to delete characters one by one, you simply place your text cursor before the first character you want to delete or after the last one (see the Information box for more about cursors). Then, if you want to delete the character after the cursor, you press the Delete key (Del) and, if you want to delete the character before the cursor, you press the Backspace key. You do this as many times as there are characters you want to delete. You can also hold down the Del or Backspace key, but, if you do this, you will need to be careful that you do not delete more characters than you intend to.

information

When you are working on a document, there are effectively two cursors on the screen. There is the mouse cursor, which looks like a capital I (with bars at the top and bottom) and this moves around the screen as you move your mouse. There is also the text cursor, which is a flashing vertical line, that shows you where in the text you are, in other words where the next thing you enter at the keyboard will take effect. You need to be clear about the difference between the two cursors.

information

For most of the time the mouse cursor does not affect what you are doing. It is only when you click with it that it plays a part. If you click the left mouse button (left click – or just click) with the mouse at any position in the text, you will move the text cursor to that position. As we will see below, there are other ways that you can move the text cursor, but the big advantage of the mouse is that you can move anywhere in the text, particularly if you also use the scroll bars. Once you have clicked, the text cursor will stay where you put it, irrespective of where you now move the mouse cursor to. If you keep the mouse button held down, then other things happen, as we shall see in the next chapter. Incidentally, if you click the right mouse button (right click), you bring up a pop-up menu that duplicates parts of the menus at the top of the Word window.

There are various other ways in which you can move the text cursor:

● You can use the arrows on the numeric keypad. There are always four (up, down, left and right) and sometimes eight of these; the additional four are diagonal (up left, up right, down left and down right). Depressing one of the first four moves your text cursor one line up or down or one character to the left or right. Depressing one of the other characters combines two movements. If you also hold down the Ctrl key, then instead of moving by a line or a character, you move by a paragraph or a line.

● You can use the Home and End keys. Home takes you to the beginning of your current line, End to the end of it. If you hold down the Ctrl key this time, Home and End will take you to the beginning or end of your document.

● You can use the Page Up and Page Down keys; these will usually take you up or down a screenful rather than a text page.

To insert a character or characters in the text, for example if you have missed a character out of a word, just place the text cursor at the position where you want to add the character(s) and type. Usually when you open Word, you will be in **Insert** mode, which means that typing will insert the new characters into the text. However, you may have switched to **Overstrike** mode, intentionally or even inadvertently, by depressing the Insert (Ins) key. If you are in

ECDL

Overstrike mode, you will find that, instead of inserting the new characters, each character replaces that to the right of the cursor as you key it; sometimes, of course, this may be what you want. If you are in Overstrike mode, then the text in the OVR box at the bottom of the window will be dark; see Figure 5.1. Note that, in Word, the text cursor does not change; in some other, particularly older, word processors, the cursor changes to a block covering the current letter (the letter is then white on black – or its colour equivalent).

Figure 5.1 The Status box in Overstrike mode.

5.3. Entering Words, Sentences and Paragraphs

To insert more than one character (in Insert mode), just keep on typing. If you want to add a new paragraph, just type at the beginning or end of an existing paragraph, adding carriage returns appropriately.

Exercise 5.3

Open the latest version of your test file. Edit it by adding additional paragraphs and words and sentences within paragraphs. Delete some text. Press the Insert key and then overtype some text. Remember to press the Insert key again to come out of Overstrike mode. Save the file as a new version (or even save as a new file, say *test03.doc*), so that you have a series of versions or files that represent the stages that you have gone through.

5.4. Inserting Symbols and Special Characters

One of the big advantage of a word processor over an old-fashioned typewriter (and there are many) is that you can include in your document many more characters than you can type directly on the keyboard. Keyboards generally used in the UK and USA are not, for example, designed so that you can key accented characters directly (unlike those used, say, in France). However, you can still key such characters, as well as all kinds of symbols. There is also a special way to key characters that have traditionally been used in printed books but not in typed documents. These include curly quote marks (' and ') and En and Em rules (– and —), as we shall see.

Exercise 5.4a

There are various ways of inserting symbols and special characters. The simplest is to go to the **Insert** menu and choose **Symbol**. A window that looks like Figure 5.2 will open (sometimes not very quickly). You can then do two things to find the symbol you want:

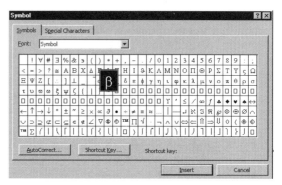

Figure 5.2 Symbol window with one character enlarged.

● Scroll through the fonts (you may also find that you can scroll through subsets); the top one is always called (normal text);

● Look at the characters; it may unfortunately take you some time to find the character you want if this is the first time you have used it.

Sometimes the characters appear rather small, but if you click on a character and hold the mouse key down, you will see a larger version of the character in question (see Figure 5.2).

To make life easier for you in some cases, you will note that in the **Symbols** window there is a second tab, labelled **Special Characters** (Figure 5.3). Here you will see listed a number of characters that occur quite frequently in well formatted material. Most of them are characters that used to be the province of the typesetter in the days when secretarial work was done on typewriters, but now they are available to everyone. Because the symbols are listed on the left, they should be self-explanatory. A few need some explanation:

★ ECDL ★

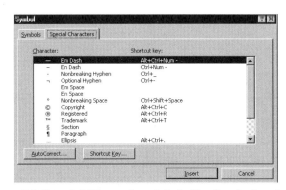

Figure 5.3 Special Characters tab in the Symbols window.

● The Em space and En spaces are fixed spaces that are the same width as the Em and En dashes above them. They are called Em and En because they are, respectively, the width of a capital M and a·capital N.

● The optional hyphen is a hyphen that only appears at the end of lines if you allow the text to be automatically hyphenated (to keep the inter-word spaces within a fixed range); see Chapter 8.

● The non-breaking space allows you to keep two words with a space between them on the same line. The non-breaking hyphen is similar.

● Your program can be set up to produce opening and closing quotes that look like ' and ' at the appropriate positions, even though you type the straight quote ' (**Format I AutoFormat As You Type I "Straight Quotes" with "Smart Quotes"**). Sometimes, however, the autoformatting gives you the wrong characters, for example when you want a single closing quote mark by itself (with a space on either side), so you can use this menu to allow you to put in the character you actually want.

You will notice that at the bottom of both the **Symbols** and **Special Characters** windows, there are two buttons, **AutoCorrect** and **Shortcut Key**. **AutoCorrect** is outside the ECDL syllabus, but allows you to automatically correct common mistakes; we shall see references to it in later chapters. If you click on it, you will see the corrections listed.

A **Shortcut Key** allows you to use a keyboard shortcut instead of the menu. This is quicker once you know the short cuts, but means you have to remember them. If, in the **Symbols** menu, you select a character and a shortcut key has already been set up, it will be displayed at the bottom right of the window (see Figure 5.2). This does not happen for the **Special Characters** window, but you can see (and change) the shortcut key by clicking the **Shortcut Key** button. Be careful, however, about using this because you may overwrite existing standard shortcut keys. Note that all the characters in the **Special Characters** window also occur in the **Symbols** window.

Another way of inserting non-keyboard characters is to use the character number, keyed on the numeric keypad while holding down the Alt key (you must have the Num Lock on). This is quite efficient, but requires you to know these numbers and effectively only applies to characters that are in the basic Windows character set (known as the ANSI character set after the American National Standards Institute), so that, for example, keying *Alt+0233* gives é. For other characters, such as those in the Symbol font, you still need to know which is the equivalent character in the ANSI character set.

Finally, for Greek characters and symbols, you can key in the character in the normal font and then change the font, as we shall see in Chapter 8. Thus keying *m* and changing the font to Symbol, as we shall see in Chapter 8, gives μ. This also applies to Cyrillic (Russian) characters, but, once you get away from alphabetical characters, remembering the equivalents becomes difficult.

Exercise 5.4b

Open one of your test files. Insert some non-alphabetical characters using the methods described previously. Add a French quotation for example and perhaps an En rule to replace a hyphen (one of the uses of En rules is to indicate a relationship, e.g. the parent–child bond). Perhaps you can consider a Greek letter to indicate an angle, say θ. See which method you find easiest to use. Again save your file or save it as *test04.doc*, for example.

5.5. Inserting a Page Break

Sometimes you want your text to continue at the top of a new page. Word allows you to insert a page break.

Exercise 5.5

Go to the **Insert** menu and select **Break**. You will see a window like Figure 5.4. **Page break** is selected by default, so all you need to do is click **OK**. Exactly what you will then see on the screen depends which layout you are using, but, if you go to **Page Layout**, you will see that the text cursor has moved to the top of the next page. In **Normal**, you see a dotted line across the page with **Page Break** typed in the middle.

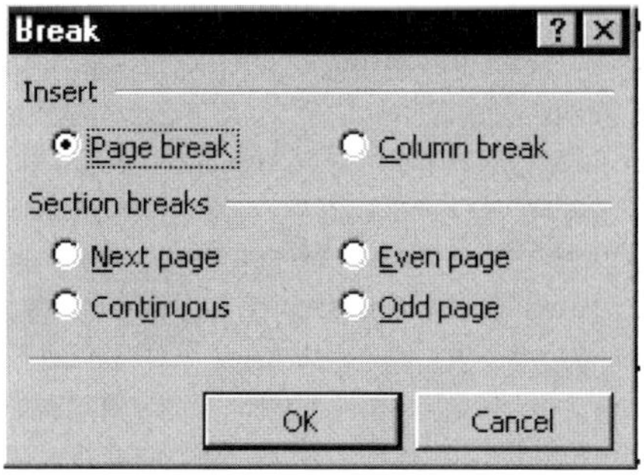

Figure 5.4 The Insert Break window.

Open your most recent test file and insert a page break at a point where it makes sense. Save the file again. (We will no longer repeat the alternative of saving as a new file, but it will be implied.)

5.6. Using Undo (and Redo)

One of the most useful commands is Undo. This is accessed from the Edit menu (or you can key Ctrl+Z or use the Toolbar icon ↶). What this does is reverse the last editing operation you carried out. Note that it does not reverse changes of view. Thus, if you have inserted some text and then decide that you did not want this, Undo will remove it without you having to delete it.

What is even more important is that Word provides multiple Undos. Thus, if you keep selecting Undo, you successively undo the operations you have carried out, in reverse order. This can sometimes be very helpful.

A related command is Redo (Ctrl+Y or toolbar icon ↷ or function key F4), which is strictly outside the ECDL syllabus but is closely linked with Undo. This allows you to repeat the last operation you carried out. It can be very useful if you want to carry out the same operation in several places in a document, particularly if this involves an operation that takes several keystrokes or a combination of keystrokes. You just move the text cursor to the new position and activate Redo.

Exercise 5.6

Note that if you use either the **Edit** menu or the keyboard shortcut (click the down arrow on the right of the symbol), you are given a clue as to what you will be **Undoing** or **Redoing**. Using the icon is actually more explicit (e.g.

Figure 5.5) and allows you to carry out several actions at one go. It is also worth noting that, if you are undoing or redoing typing, you need to check carefully exactly how much text has been affected.

Figure 5.5

So open your latest test file. Try carrying some edits and undoing and redoing them. Look at what the toolbar icon tells you rather than always using Ctrl+Z or Ctrl+Y (F4).

Summary

In this chapter:

● We have looked at inserting, overwriting and deleting characters.
● We have looked at inserting symbols and special characters.
● We have looked at inserting a page break.
● We have looked at using Undo and Redo.

Selecting, Copying, Moving and Deleting Data

6

In this chapter you will learn how to

- *Select text.*
- *Copy and moving text within and between documents.*
- *Delete text.*

6.1. Introduction

One real advantage of a word processor over a typewriter is that you can use text over and over again by copying it and you can move it around very easily. Here we shall see how you do that, as well as how you can delete it.

6.2. Selecting text

If you want to carry out an action on a piece of text, which can be anything from a single character to the whole text of your document, the first thing you need to do is to select it. As for many tasks in Word, there is more than one way to do this.

Exercise 6.1

Open your latest test file and try the following methods of selecting text:

● To select the complete text, open the **Edit** menu and choose **Select All**. Even easier is to use the keyboard shortcut and type Ctrl+A. The text will change to reverse video, i.e. negative white on black (if you are using black type on a white background as in Figure 6.1; otherwise the colours will change).

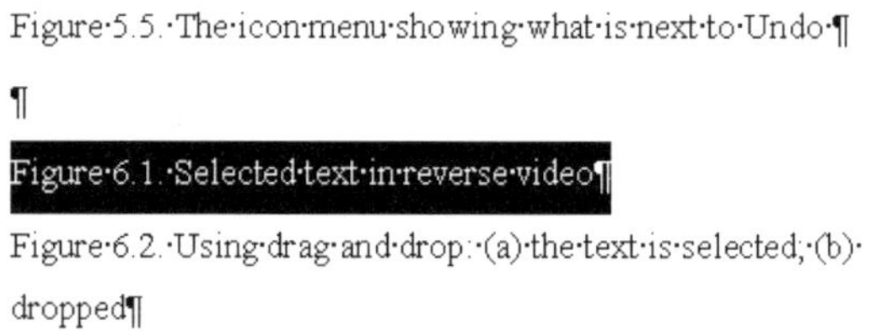

Figure·5.5.·The·icon·menu·showing·what·is·next·to·Undo·¶

¶

Figure·6.1.·Selected·text·in·reverse·video¶

Figure·6.2.·Using·drag·and·drop:·(a)·the·text·is·selected;·(b)· dropped¶

Figure 6.1 Selected text in reverse video.

● Place the cursor (the mouse cursor) at the beginning of the text you want to select and, holding down the left button, move the cursor to the end of the text you want and release.

● Place the cursor (the mouse cursor) at the beginning of the text you want to select, click and hold down the Shift key. Move to the end of the text you want to select and click again; you can go up or down the document. If you have to scroll, i.e. the beginning and end of the text you want do not appear on the screen at the same time, then this is much easier than holding down the mouse button while you scroll. You can also use this approach to extend a selection, but only in the direction in which the selection was originally made.

● To select a single word, click once on that word. If you double-click, you will select the whole paragraph. If you click once while holding down the Ctrl key, then you will select the sentence.

● Use the arrow keys and the Home and End keys. You will remember that these move you around the document. If you hold down the Shift key at the same time as you press one of these keys, you will select from the position of the text cursor. Thus shift plus a single arrow selects a single character (left and right arrows) or a single line (up and down arrows), while holding down Ctrl as well selects words or paragraphs. Shift+Home selects from the text cursor position to the beginning of the line and Shift+End selects from the text cursor position to the end of the line (including the carriage return if there is one). Holding down Ctrl as well selects to the beginning or end of the document (and also takes you to the beginning or end of the document).

● Use the function key F8. Click once on F8 and the (mouse) cursor will now select when you click. Click again and you will extend the selection. Click within the selection and you will shorten the selection. Pressing F8 again has a similar effect. Pressing F8 together with Shift reduces the selection. To 'switch off' F8, press the Escape key (Esc).

To deselect text selected by clicking or double clicking, you just click on it again. If you have selected text by using a combination of keys (Home, End or arrow keys), you can deselect part of the text. You hold down the shift key and click at the point where you want the deselection to end. This works from the end of the selection if you selected the earlier point in the document first, and from the beginning if you selected the later point in the document first. You can also use F8, by itself or together with the cursor.

You will find that you develop your own preferred way of selecting text. Once you start using Word in earnest, selecting text will be something you do all the time.

Although at the moment you will be doing nothing with what you select, try to familiarise yourself with the various approaches and see which you find easiest. For example, some people think that using F8 is a great approach, while others find it confusing. See what you think.

6.3. Copying and Moving Text

In principle, the easiest way to move text is to use drag and drop. That is, you select some text and then, holding down the mouse button, you drag the text until it is where you want it, when you release the mouse button (Figure 6.2). However, this is generally only easy if the amount of text is not too large or you are dragging within what you can see on the screen. While you can drag and drop off the screen by moving the cursor to the edge of the screen, what happens then is not always easy to control.

Figure·6.2·Using·drag·and·drop· (a)·the·text·is·selected ·(b)·drag·and·drop·in·progress,·(c)·the·text·has·been· dropped¶

Figure 6.2 Selecting text for drag and drop editing.

If you have a window open on the screen, such as Find or Replace (see Chapter 7), you cannot drag and drop text.

Drag and drop allows you to move text. However, if you hold down the Ctrl key when you drag and drop, then you will copy the selected text. However, an alternative method is necessary for copying and moving large amounts of text (and can, of course, be used for short selections as well). This uses what is called the Clipboard and techniques called Copy, Cut and Paste.

6.4. The Clipboard, Copy, Cut and Paste

To copy text from one place in a document to another or indeed between documents, you first select what you want to copy and then choose **Copy**, either from the **Edit** menu or from the pop-up menu you see when you right click on your selection. What happens then, although this is not obvious from what you see on the screen, is that the text you have selected is stored (usually described as placed) on the Clipboard, which you can think of as a special area in the computer memory. The term Clipboard is used because, if you think of the physical analogy, you can take a piece of paper and add it to a clipboard until you decide where it should be pasted back in.

If you decide that, instead of copying some text, you want to move it, then instead of choosing **Copy** from the **Edit** menu or the pop-up menu, you choose **Cut**. This time the text will vanish. Again it has been copied to the Clipboard. In either case, you then move to where you want to place the text you have copied or cut. This can either be within the same document or within a different document. To move between open documents you go the **Window** menu and select the document you want (see Chapter 2). You can even open a completely new document to paste your text into.

★ ★ ★
★ ★
★ ECDL ★
★ ★
★ ★ ★

To paste the text back into the document, you either go to the
Edit menu or right click at the position where you want to paste and
select **Paste**. The text will then appear. You may have to adjust the
typeface or typesize (Chapter 8) to match the new position. You
should also check the inter-word spacing (and possibly the number of
carriage returns), before and after the passage you pasted in to make
sure that you have neither left no space nor left a double space (or
carriage return).

information

> **Note that it is not just text you can copy, cut and paste.**
> **Module 2 discusses moving and copying files, but you can**
> **also copy and move illustrations. And you are not limited**
> **to copying within an application. So you can copy and**
> **move text and illustrations from or to, for example, an**
> **Excel file in an Excel application window (see Chapter 17).**
> **The other thing to note is that the Clipboard will retain an**
> **object (file name, text picture etc.) until either you turn**
> **your computer off or you carry out another Cut or Copy**
> **operation. Thus, you can Paste the contents of the**
> **Clipboard in more than one place (this can be very useful**
> **with text), but remember that if you do cut or copy**
> **something else, then what was previously on the Clipboard**
> **is lost. Of course, if you copied, then this is not a problem.**
> **However, if you are cutting, then you need to be careful,**
> **although you can use Undo to reverse a Cut, which is**
> **sometimes very useful if you Cut when you meant to Copy!**
> **It is possible to obtain programs that allow more than one**
> **item to be retained on the Clipboard and, indeed, Windows**
> **2000 itself allows a few items to be retained.**

The keyboard shortcuts for Cut, Copy and Paste are probably some of
the most widely used. They are (with their icons):

● **Cut** ✂ : Ctrl+X

● **Copy** 📋 : Ctrl+C

● **Paste** 📋 : Ctrl+V

You will note that, along with Ctrl+Z (Undo), they are at the
bottom left of the (UK) keyboard and, even for one-finger typists,
are easy to access.

It is also worth repeating that all the move and copy operations can be reversed with Undo (Ctrl+Z).

Exercise 6.4

Open your latest test file. Select passages by whatever method you found easiest in the previous exercise and then see what happens when you **Cut** them or **Copy** them and then **Paste** them elsewhere in your document. You can also try dragging and dropping (with and without holding down Ctrl) and compare the ease with which this can be done for a word, a sentence and a paragraph.

6.5. Deleting Text

Deleting files is similar to copying and moving, except that once you have selected the text you want to remove, you either click the right mouse button or you go to the **File** menu of the window containing the file(s) you want to delete and select **Delete**. Even simpler is just to depress the Del (delete) key on your keyboard. You can, of course, also delete by using the Delete and Backspace keys without previously selecting any text.

Exercise 6.5

Repeat the last exercise, although this time delete some of the text you select. You can always use **Undo** to restore it.

This is probably a good point at which to review your test document and check that the text makes some sense. All the changes you have made may have moved it away from what you originally intended. You can, of course, simply revert to an earlier version. Did you save versions of the test document?

Summary

In this chapter:

- We have looked at ways of selecting text.
- We have looked at moving and copying text within a document, using either drag and drop or Cut, Copy and Paste, together with the Clipboard.
- We have looked at deleting text.

Searching
and Replacing

- *Search for characters or text strings.*
- *Replace characters or text strings with other characters.*

7.1. Introduction

You will often want to find a word or phrase in a document, either when you are writing and you want to see what you have already put or when you are reading or editing a document. When you are writing, or perhaps editing or revising, a document, you may also want to replace a string of characters, for example January by February. Word provides you with very extensive facilities for doing this. We shall only describe the simpler aspects here.

7.2. Finding Characters

There is a special **Find** menu (Figure 7.1a), which you can open from the **Edit** menu or by keying Ctrl+F. To find a string of characters, you simply type them into the box and click on **Find Next** (or key Alt+F). If the string exists in the document, then the next occurrence will be highlighted. If the string does not exist in the document or you have found all the occurrences, you will see a message telling you so.

Figure 7.1a The Find window – basic.

In Figure 7.1a you will see a button labelled **More**. If you click on this, the window expands so that it looks like Figure 7.1b. You will see various boxes, representing options:

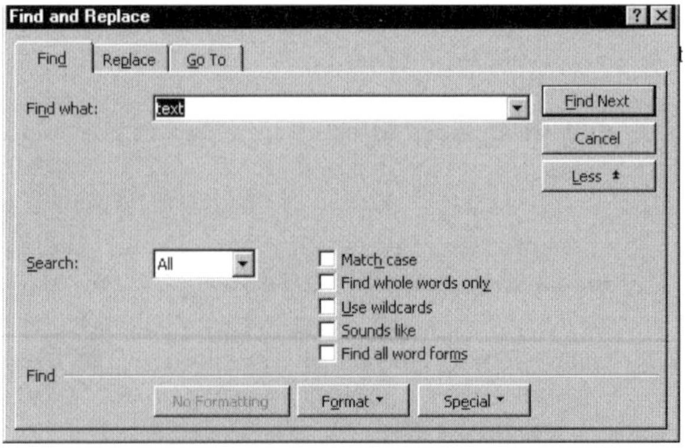

Figure 7.1b The Find window – expanded.

★ ECDL ★

● **Search**: this can say **All**, **Down** or **Up**. If you select **Down**, you will search from the present position of your text cursor to the end of the document. Correspondingly, with **Up** selected you will search back to the beginning, while with **All**, as you would expect, the search goes through the whole document, going to the end and then starting again at the beginning until it gets back to the original position of the text cursor. If you select **Up** or **Down**, Word, unlike some other programs, tells you that it has reached the beginning or end of the document and gives you the option to search the rest of the document.

● **Match case**: unless this box is selected, a search will find all occurrences of a string, irrespective of whether it contains capital or small letters. If you select this box, you will only find occurrences corresponding to the case you enter. Thus if this box is selected and you search for 'brown' you will not find occurrences of 'Brown'. Similarly, if you search for 'Brown', you will not find 'brown'.

● **Find whole words only**: if this is selected, searching for 'can', for example, will not find 'scan', or 'candidate'.

● **Use wildcards**: This allows you to search for more complex strings, for example all strings beginning in 'is' and continuing with a, e or i, so that one can change them to -isa, ise or -isi, depending on the style that you are using. However, this is outside the scope of ECDL. Word has some very powerful string searching capabilities, which are described in the Help files, but you need to understand the principles before you try to use these.

● **Sounds like**: this finds words that sound like the search term that you have entered. You have to allow for US pronunciation when you use this option.

● **Find all word forms**: if this is selected, when you search for, say, 'stay', you will also find 'stays', 'staying', 'stayed' etc.

At the bottom of the screen, you will also see three buttons, **No formatting**, **Format** and **Special**. The first cancels the second, which allows you to add all kinds of conditions to your search, e.g. the characters have to be italic or bold or in a particular typeface. This is outside the scope of ECDL, but is well explained in the Help files.

The **Special** button is useful as it allows you to search for things other than just letters; see Figure 7.2, which is self-explanatory.

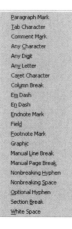

Figure 7.2 Special characters you can specify in Find.

Exercise 7.2

Open your latest test file (or perhaps an earlier version that you want to clean up). Search for words or strings that you know are there and, just to see what happens, words or strings that you know are not there. Try out the different search options to see their effect.

7.3. Replacing Characters

In Figure 7.1, you will see that there are two other tabs, **Replace** and **Go To**. You can access these by clicking once you are in **Find** or you can get to them directly from the **Edit** menu. **Replace**, strictly speaking **Find and Replace**, can also be accessed from the keyboard shortcut Ctrl+H.

Exercise 7.3a

The **Replace** menu looks like Figure 7.3a and, like **Find**, it can be expanded by using the **More** button (Figure 7.3b). You will see that it is very like the **Find** menu, except that it has a **Replace with** box and additional buttons, **Replace** and **Replace All**. The selectable options all work in the same way as for **Find**, although, if you use **Special Characters** when the text cursor is in the **Replace** box, you will see that the list is different and shorter (Figure 7.4). Comparison of Figures 7.2 and 7.4 will show you why. It does not make sense, for example, to replace with any number, although you may well wish to search for any number.

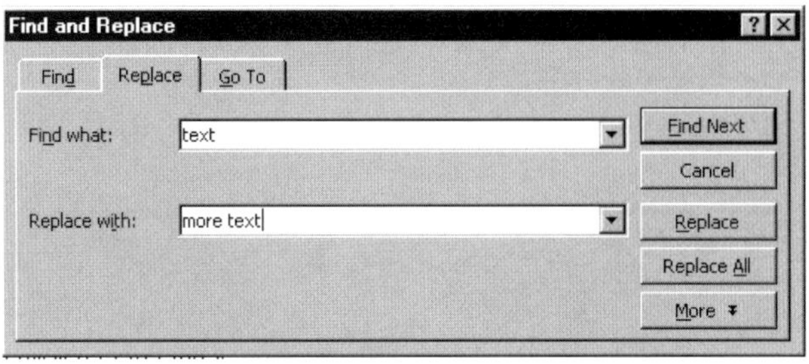

●●●●●●●❼●●●●●●●●●●●●●

Figure 7.3a The Replace window – basic.

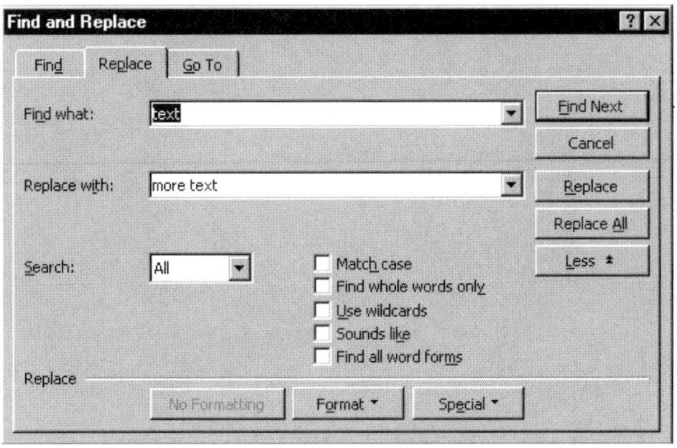

Figure 7.3b The Replace window – expanded.

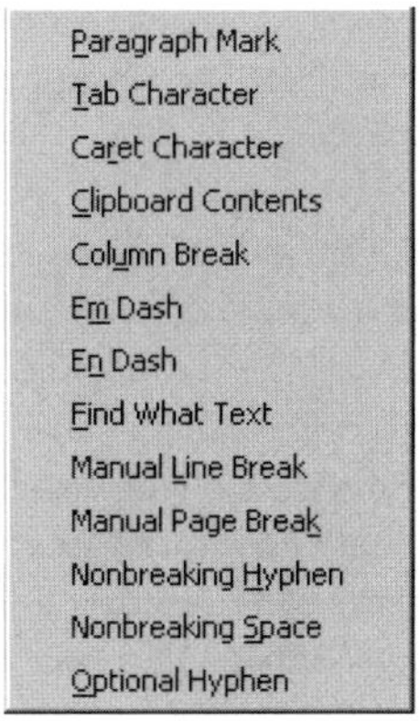

Figure 7.4 Special characters in Replace.

If you enter text in the **Find what** and **Replace with** boxes, say 'cats' in **Find what** and 'dogs' in **Replace with**, then, if you click the **Replace** button, you will replace the first instance of 'cats' with 'dogs' and highlight the next instance (or Word will tell you that the whole document has been searched). Clicking the **Replace** button again will repeat the process. If you click **Replace All**, however, every instance of 'cats' in a document will be replaced by 'dogs'.

You need to be careful when using Replace, because searching for 'can', for example, and replacing it with 'could' will not only change 'can' to 'could', but also 'scan' to 'scould', which you will not want. Thus, you can either select the 'Find whole words only' option or enter the string with spaces, e.g. ' can', but the latter would also change 'canvas', while putting a space at the end would mean that you would not find examples of 'can' followed by punctuation. It is therefore important to think about what you are doing!

Exercise 7.3b

Now replace words, characters and strings with other words, characters and strings in your test document. One very useful replacement is to replace all double spaces with single spaces; you can repeat this until you get a zero result, when you will no longer have any double spaces in your document. Try using the **Special Characters** in the **Find** and **Replace** boxes. You can always use **Undo** if you wish. Alternatively, when you close the file, you can decide not to save the changes.

Although traditionally, secretarial usage is to put a double space after a full stop, you will find that this does not normally happen in typeset material. You need to decide which approach you are going to take.

Remember that when you use Find or Replace, the Browse object (see Section 2.3 and Figure 2.11) will change to what you last looked for.

7.4. Using Go To

Although not within the ECDL syllabus, the **Go To** command appears together with Find and Replace. It appears as shown in Figure 7.5 and is self-explanatory. It is most useful when editing a document, rather than when you are writing a new one. The keyboard shortcut is Ctrl+G.

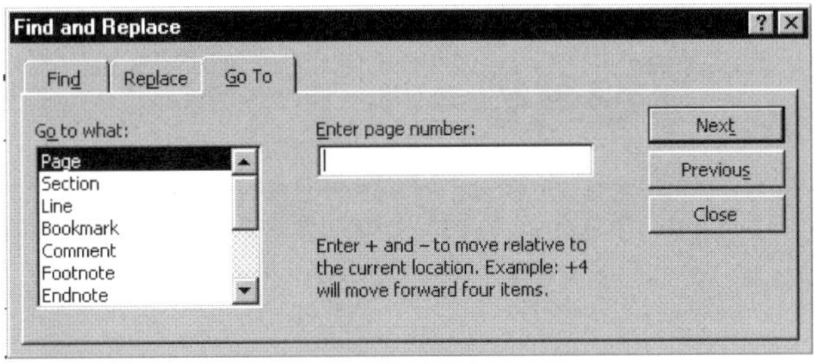

Figure 7.5 The Go To window.

Summary

In this chapter:

- We have looked at how to use Find.
- We have looked at how to use Replace.
- We have looked at how to use Go To.

8

Text
Formatting

In this chapter you will learn how to

Format text, including changing the typeface, type size, style (italic, bold and underlining), the colour and the alignment.

Format paragraphs, including changing the alignment (left, right centre and justified), using hyphenation if appropriate, indenting, changing the line spacing and other characteristics.

Copy the formatting from a selected piece of text to another.

★ ECDL ★

●●●●●●●●⑧●●●●●●●●●●●

8.1. Introduction

In many ways what we shall look at in this chapter is at the heart of word processing, how you actually make your document look the way you want it to. Chapters 9 to 11 cover other aspects, but here we deal with the basics in terms of getting the characters and paragraphs to look the way you want them to.

8.2. Formatting Fonts

What is a font? The term derives from the days when metal type was used and had to be cast, the French word being fonde. In fact, British usage was generally 'fount', rather than font, but US usage has taken over with the spread of computers. There has also been some disagreement over exactly what a font is. Does it include the size or just the typeface? Are italic and bold of the same typeface the same font or not? However, these arguments are all rather sterile, so here we shall refer to typeface and type size, with italic, bold etc. referred to as font style where we need a generic term.

The basic choice of typeface and type size is usually controlled from the toolbar. Figure 8.1 shows the drop-down menu for typefaces. Those at the top, above the double line, are the fonts you are currently using in your present editing session, while the remainder are listed in alphabetical order. The icon on the left of the font name describes how the font is encoded, but for the purposes of ECDL you do not need to know about that, except that fonts with the TrueType **T** icon will always appear on your printer exactly as shown on the screen. The others (here the typefaces are called PostScript, but the Icon represents Adobe Type Manager – or ATM – which is the software used to represent them on screen) may or may not appear as shown on the screen, depending whether they are downloaded from your system or stored on your printer. Certainly, if the typeface appears in this list, you can use it in your document. To use a typeface for a particular piece of text, you select that text and then go to the list of faces and click on the one you want to use.

Figure 8.1 The typeface drop-down menu.

Similarly, Figure 8.2 shows the type-size drop-down list. Again you select the text you want to change and click on the size you want. If the size you want is not shown, simply type it in the box at the top and type Enter. Type sizes are given in points, which is a long-standing typographic unit. Word allows you to specify type size to a precision of half a point, but not more precisely (unlike page make-up programs). If you really want to, you can go up to a size of 999 points and, in practice, 6 or 7 point type is about the smallest that is comfortable to read.

Figure 8.2 The type-size drop-down menu.

You can also set the font style from the toolbar (italic, bold or underline – see Figure 8.3), whilst the corresponding keyboard shortcuts are Ctrl+I, Ctrl+B and Ctrl+U. These are what is described as toggle commands, so that if your original selection is not italic, then keying Ctrl+I or selecting the appropriate icon will make it italic. Similarly if your selected text is already italic, keying Ctrl+I or selecting the appropriate icon will remove the italic style. Note that, if you select

★ ★ ★
★ ★
★ ECDL ★
★ ★
★ ★ ★

a sentence that begins in italic, but is not fully italic throughout, then clicking the italic icon or keying Ctrl+I will remove all the italics. In contrast, if the sentence had begun not in italic, but included some italics, then clicking the italic icon or keying Ctrl+I will make the whole sentence italic. The bold and underline commands work in the same way, although all three are independent and can be combined.

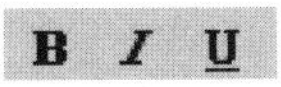

Figure 8.3 Font style icons on the toolbar.

Exercise 8.2

More detailed font formatting is controlled by the Font Format menu. Go to the **Format** menu and select **Font**. You will see a window that looks like Figure 8.4. First, you can see that it is possible to set the typeface, type-size and font style. You can also set the colour from the **Color** drop-down menu and a variety of what Word calls **Effects**, which are fairly self-explanatory. You will also see a sample of the font and a brief explanation of the type of font (which corresponds to the icon in the font listing). Once you have made your choice, you click **OK** in the usual way.

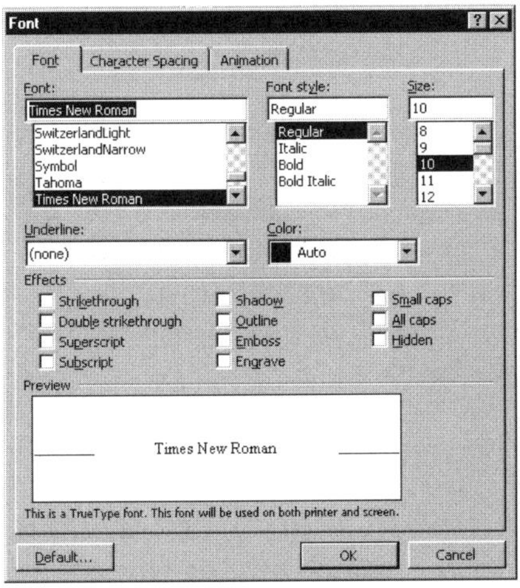

Figure 8.4 The Font Format window.

You will see that the Font Format window has two other tabs, **Animation**, which you can ignore for the purposes of ECDL, particularly if you are solely involved in producing printed documents. **Character spacing** is more important. The window (Figure 8.5) contains four lines:

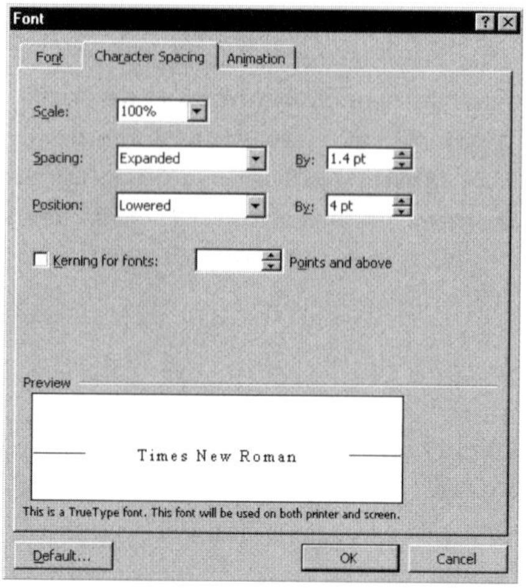

Figure 8.5 Character spacing tab in the Font Format window.

● **Scale** allows you to change the typesize within a line without changing the inter-line spacing (which is related to the main font size, but can be changed in the paragraph format window, as discussed below).

● **Spacing** allows you to contract or expand the spacing between characters. It can be useful for fitting text into a limited space for example.

● **Position** allows you to move characters up and down relative to the base line (the line that is formed by the bases of the letters without descenders, i.e. not letters such as p, q, y and g). Note that for subscripts and superscripts it often looks better if you use the subscript and superscript options (**Effects**) in the main font window because these also reduce the character size, rather than just moving the characters relative to the base line.

● **Kerning** is changing the inter-character spacing between certain characters for aesthetic reasons. A good example is the space between A and W (AW), which if not kerned looks disproportionately large. You do not usually need to make any adjustments here as it happens automatically.

Now open the latest version of your test file. You can start to make it look better. Try changing the typeface and the type size until you find a combination that you like. You may notice that some faces look larger, even though they are nominally the same size as others. You may also want to add bold or italics (adding underlines is not generally regarded as good style, but add them if you wish). **Save** the file when you like what you have.

information

Typefaces come in two main types, called serif and sanserif (or sometimes sans-serif). In French sans means 'without', so serif faces have serifs and sanserif faces do not. Serifs are the small 'hooks' at the end of the strokes that make up letters. Thus, Times is a serif face, whereas Helvetica (used here for Exercises) is not. Can you see the difference?

8.3. Formatting Paragraphs

Again, you can set some paragraph formatting from the toolbar. For example, Figure 8.6 shows the icons you can use to adjust the text alignment:

Figure 8.6 Paragraph alignment icons on the toolbar.

This paragraph has been left aligned. You will notice that the right-hand side is 'ragged', i.e. not justified, and the text is not hyphenated, so that if a word will not fit, it is taken over to the next line. This means that the interword spacing is always the same.

This text has been right aligned. You will notice that the left-hand side is now 'ragged', i.e. not justified, and the text is not hyphenated, so that if a word will not fit, it is taken over to the next line. This means that the interword spacing is still always the same.

This text has been centred. You will notice that the both sides are now 'ragged', i.e. not justified, and the text is not hyphenated, so that if a word will not fit, it is taken over to the next line. This means that the interword spacing is always the same.

This text has been justified, and indented on both sides, partly to distinguish it from the main text. You will notice that both sides are now justified, but not hyphenated, so that if a word will not fit, it is taken over to the next line. This means that the interword spacing varies. However, if there are long words, such as antidisestablishmentarianism, intergovernmental or pseudointellectual, and/or if the line length is short, some of the interword spaces can be quite large.

From the toolbar, you can also adjust the indent (see Figure 8.7).

Figure 8.7 Indentation icons on the toolbar.

We shall now see how to deal with these large spaces by selecting hyphenation in the paragraph format menu.

Exercise 8.3a

Open the paragraph format window by going to the **Format** menu and selecting **Paragraph**. The **Indents and Spacings** tab (Figure 8.8) allows you to adjust the alignment and indents as in the justified example above and also the general paragraph layout:

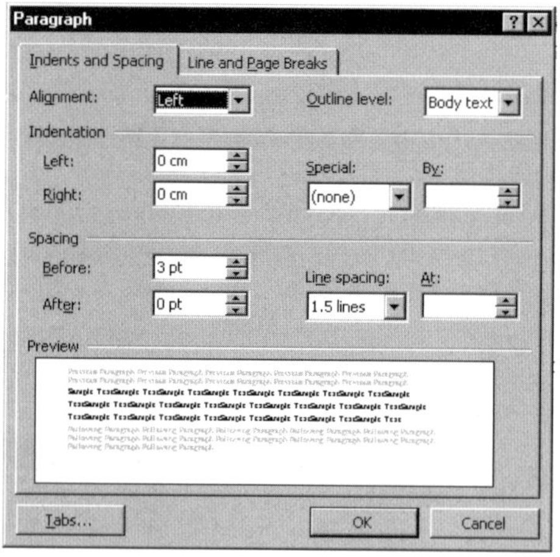

Figure 8.8 Paragraph format window: Indents and Spacing tab.

● **Alignment** allows the same options as the toolbar (Figure 8.6).

● The **Outline level** relates to what you see in the Outline view of the document, but is not covered in the ECDL syllabus.

● **Left and right indentation** are self-explanatory; note that you can only generally set left indents from the toolbar.

● **Special indentation** has two options. **Hanging** indents all lines except the first by the amount specified, while **First line** indents only the first line by the amount specified.

● **Spacing before and after** specifies the amount of spacing before and after the paragraph.

● **Line spacing** allows you various options (see Figure 8.9). The **At:** box only comes into effect if you choose **Exactly**, **At least** or **Multiple**.

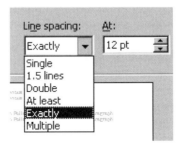

Figure 8.9 Line spacing options.

Again you can see a preview and can click **OK** if you are happy. Note that making these changes only affects the current paragraph. You only have to have the text cursor placed somewhere within the paragraph for the changes to apply; you do not have to select the whole paragraph. Alternatively, you can select a number of paragraphs to which the changes are to apply.

The other tab in this window is **Line and Page Breaks** (Figure 8.10). The Page break options are:

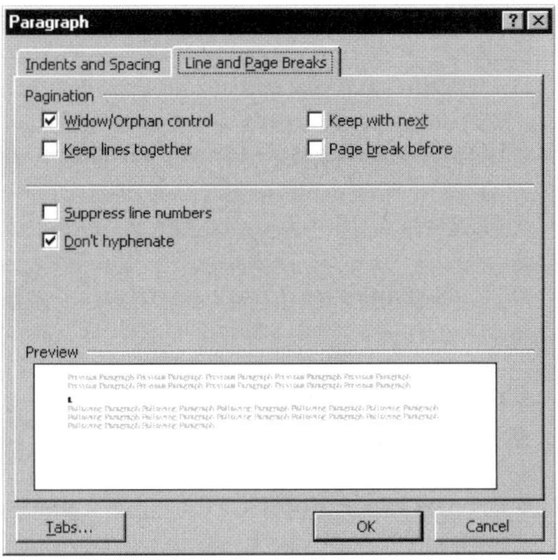

Figure 8.10 Line and Page Breaks tab.

- **Widow and Orphan control**. If selected, this stops odd lines being left at the top and bottom of pages. In Word you cannot control the minimum number of lines, as you can in some programs.

- **Keep with next**. If selected, the paragraph will always be on the same page as the one following. Note that it only makes sense to use this occasionally, for example with headings, as otherwise you can have some very short pages or not even be able to paginate at all.

- **Keep lines together**. If selected, all the paragraph will be included on one page.

- **Page break before**. This is self-explanatory.

The other two options in this window are:

- **Suppress line numbers**. For this to have any effect, you have to indicate that you want line numbering as default. You do this in the **File** menu and choose **Page Setup** and then the **Layout** tab (Section 13.3).

- **Don't Hyphenate**. Again, for this to have any effect, you have to have hyphenation set for the whole document. You do this in the **Tools** menu, selecting **Languages and Hyphenation**, where you can also set the parameters that control when hyphenation takes place.

If you have hyphenation set, the paragraph given above (with the text changed appropriately) now looks like:

> This text has been justified, and indented on both sides, partly to dis-
> tinguish it from the main text. You will notice that the both sides are now
> justified and now hyphenated, so that if a word will not fit, it is hyphen-
> ated, rather than taken to the next line. This means that the interword
> spacing varies. However, if there are long words, such as antidisestab-
> lishmentarianism, intergovernmental or pseudointellectual, and/or if the
> line length is short, some of the interword spaces are now not so large.
> If you do not like the hyphenation breaks, you can add optional
> hyphens (see Chapter 5).

Exercise 8.3b

Now continue the operation with your test file and add some formatting to your paragraphs. As your test file is a letter, the address and the date should probably be aligned right. You may also want to change the interline spacing in the paragraphs and perhaps the spacing before and after the paragraphs. Do you need spacing before and after? You may also want to add some indents.

●●●●●●●⑧●●●●●●●●●●

8.4. Copying Formats

There may be times when you want to copy the character or paragraph format of one piece of text to another piece. To do this you use the **Format Painter** icon on the toolbar. This is one of the few commands that does not exist in the menus:

Exercise 8.4

1. You select the text from which you want to copy the format.

2. You click the **Format Painter** . Double click if you want to copy the formatting to more than one location. The cursor will change shape.

3. Select the (first) text to which you want to copy the format. If you only clicked (rather than double clicked) on **Format Painter**, the reformatting will take place and the cursor will change back to normal.

4. If you double clicked on **Format Painter**, click on the next section that you want reformatted. Do this as many times as is necessary.

5. Click on **Format Painter** to cancel when you have finished.

6. Continue the operation with the test file and copy the style from one paragraph to another. Save when you are happy.

Summary

In this chapter:

● We have looked at how to format characters.
● We have looked at how to format paragraphs.
● We have looked at how to copy formatting using the Format Painter

General Formatting: Tabs, Lists and Borders

9

In this chapter you will learn how to

- *Use and set tabs.*
- *Use lists.*
- *Add borders to your document.*

★ ECDL ★

9.1. Introduction

Some information is much more understandable if it is laid out as a table or list. Here we shall look at using tab markers and list commands to align text. Fully formatted tables will be covered in Chapter 15. Adding a border or box to all or some of the information can also make it clearer. We shall cover that here too.

9.2. Using and Setting Tab Markers

There are four different tab markers you can set so that the text aligns to the left, to the centre, to the right and to a decimal point. You can use these to set simple tables, although more complex tables are better handled with table formatting (Chapter 15). Aligning to a tab marker is very similar to aligning the paragraph text as we saw in Chapter 8, except that you can define alignment points (tab markers) at any point in a paragraph. Figure 9.1 illustrates the four different tab settings.

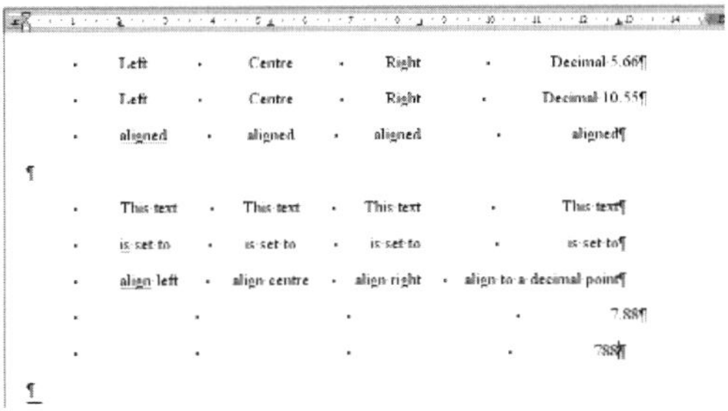

Figure 9.1 Tab settings.

It is important to understand that tabs apply line by line. The text at the top of Figure 9.1 is keyed in the following order: <tab>*Left* <tab>*Centre* <tab>*Right* <tab>*Decimal 5.66* <cr><tab>*Left* <tab>*Centre* etc. (<tab> means a tab character produced by striking the Tab key and <cr> means a carriage return produced by striking Enter.) The text in the lower part of figure is typed in the order: <tab>*This text* <tab>*This text* <tab>*This text* <tab>*This text* <cr><tab>*is set to* <tab>*is set to* <tab>*is set to* <tab>*is set to* <cr><tab>*align left.* <tab>*align centrally.* <tab>*align right.* <tab>*align to a decimal point.* <cr><tab> <tab> <tab> <tab>*7.88* <cr><tab> <tab> <tab> <tab>*788.* Note that with a decimal tab any line that does not include a decimal point or full stop will align as though the decimal point is at the end (just as though it were a number).

This may look a little confusing, but it is important to understand that while tab characters are ideal for aligning short pieces of text or numbers, they are not a good way to align paragraphs that spread over more than one line. This is because you have to key the text line by line and if, for example, you decide to change the typesize of your document (or even the typeface), you may find that your text no longer fits and has to be rekeyed, which is something best avoided.

information

> **Although we are referring here to the decimal point as a full stop, the character to be used as a decimal point (along with various related settings) can be set differently in the Control Panel | Regional Settings (see Section 2). The French, for example, generally use the comma as a decimal point.**

If you look at Figure 9,1, on the ruler above each alignment point you can see where the tab stop (or tab marker) has been set, with the shape telling you what kind of tab stop it is. (It is known as a tab stop because in the days of the typewriter this was physically a stop that prevented the carriage moving further, though there were only left tab stops in those days.) The L shape is a left stop, the inverted T a centre stop, the reversed L a right stop and the inverted T followed by a decimal point a decimal tab.

Exercise 9.2

You set these points (tab stops) in stages (note that setting tabs involves two types of operation, setting the position and inserting the tab character in the text):

step **1.** Type a line (or lines) of text and insert tabs before the text you want to align. At this stage the text will probably align to a series of default positions (which do not appear as tabs on the ruler) – see the text at the end of this exercise.

step **2.** Click on the box to the left of the ruler until it shows the type of tab stop you want to set. The settings indicator rotates as you click (**Left**, **Centre**, **Right**, **Decimal**, etc.).

step **3.** Make sure that the text cursor is in the paragraph in which you want to set a tab. This may sound obvious, but is very easy to overlook. You can, of course, select a number of paragraphs and the settings will apply to all of them.

step **4.** Click on the menu bar at the position(s) where you want the tab stop(s). If you need more than one type of tab stop, then you will have to repeat stage 1 between each click. However, you can set all the left tabs first and then ull the decimal tabs, for example. You do not have to work from right to left. You will find that the tab stop may not go exactly to the position you want, locking on to an invisible grid. To place the stop exactly, you can hold down the Alt key as you adjust the position. As you set each tab stop, you will see the text align. If you are unhappy with any of the tab stops, you can either drag and drop them along the bar (holding down the Alt key if necessary) or drag and drop them off the bar altogether to remove them. Note that, if the text goes past a tab stop, then that tab stop will be ignored.

If you are keying in a paragraph with the tab stops set and you key a carriage return, then the settings will also apply to the new paragraph you have created.

As we have seen in Step 1, if you have no tab stops set, you will find that keying tabs still aligns the text to a series of default positions. The spacing of these can be set, as discussed in the next section.

information

You can change the units of measurement you are using by going to the Tools menu and selecting Options and then General. At the bottom, you will see a window where you change between inches, centimetres, picas and points.

9.3. Formatting Tabs

Instead of using your mouse and setting tabs by eye, you can go to the **Format** menu and select **Tabs**. A window like that shown in Figure 9.2 will open.

Tabs ? X

Tab stop position:
5.25 cm

| 2 cm |
| 5.25 cm |
| 8.5 cm |
| 12.75 cm |

Default tab stops: 1.27 cm

Alignment
- ○ Left
- ● Center
- ○ Right
- ○ Decimal
- ○ Bar

Leader
- ● 1 None
- ○ 2 ......
- ○ 3 -------
- ○ 4 ____

Tab stops to be cleared:

Set | Clear | Clear All

OK | Cancel

Figure 9.2 The Tab Format window.

93

Perhaps the first box to note is at the top right, **Default tab stops**. Here you can adjust spacing of the default tab stop positions, repeated across the page at the interval shown in the box; these can be useful if you want the same alignment throughout your document. You can adjust the spacing value by keying in a new figure or clicking on the up or down arrow at the side of the box. However, as soon as you set just one tab stop in a paragraph, the default positions no longer apply.

Near the bottom of the window you will see three buttons, **Set**, **Clear** and **Clear All**. If there are no tab stops shown in the box on the left, then you type the position where you want to set the tab into the box at the top left. You can overwrite what is already there, because it is just a copy of what is in the larger box below. Select the type of tab stop you want and click on **Set**. You can do this as many time as you want. When you have finished, click **OK**. If you just set one stop, you can skip clicking on **Set** and just click **OK**. However, if you set more than one stop, you must click **Set** after keying each position except the last. Note that you can also select the alignment of each stop. Just as with setting stops on the ruler, the new tab positions will apply to the current paragraph or all the paragraphs selected.

You will notice that there is an additional type of alignment called **bar**. If you set this, you will find that you get a vertical bar, the height of the paragraph, at the tab stop position. However, this is not a real tab stop because the tab key does not recognise the position (even though a vertical bar also appears on the ruler which makes the bar easy to move or remove). So if you want text aligning to the left of a bar, you need to set the bar and a right tab stop just before it.

Before you click set, you can also set a **Leader** character. This means that, instead of space between the text aligned at the different tab stops, you get whatever leader character you specify. Figure 9.3 repeats Figure 9.1 with Leaders and bar stops included.

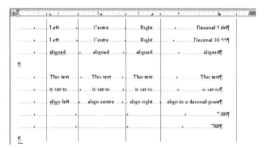

Figure 9.3 Tab settings with leaders and bars.

To remove stops, you open the **Tab format** window and select the tab you want to remove by clicking on the setting in the large box. The setting will then be copied to the smaller box above. Click **Clear** and that tab stop will no longer apply to the current paragraph (or any paragraphs selected). If you want to get rid of all the stops, just click on **Clear All**.

> **Although you can move tab stops on the ruler, you cannot edit tab stop positions in the Tab format window. You have to clear a stop and enter a new stop in a new position.**

Exercise 9.3a

In this exercise, you will repeat what you did in Exercise 9.2, but this time use the tab formatting box.

1. Type a line (or lines) of text (or take some text you have already keyed) and insert tabs before the text you want to align. At this stage, as before, the text will probably align to a series of default positions or to any tab positions you have previously set.

2. Make sure that the text cursor is in the paragraph in which you want to set a tab. You can again, of course, select a number of pargraphs and the settings will apply to all of them.

3. Go to **Format I Tabs**. If any tab positions are showing, then click on **Clear All** to get rid of them.

4. By reference to the ruler at the top of the text area, decide the positions of the tab stops you want to add.

5. Add tab stops (and their alignments) as described above, clicking **Set** between each one and **OK** when you have finished. You will then see that the tab stops have appeared on the ruler at the top of the type area.

Exercise 9.3b

Open the latest version of your test document and add some information with tab stops included. Perhaps you could add information about when you started each ECDL module or how long each chapter took you (include a decimal tab). Try adding leaders and bar stops. Once you have set up the tabs, try adjusting them (with and without the Alt key held down). Save the version you are happy with.

9.4. Lists

A different way of aligning text is to use a list. Figure 9.4 shows a bulleted list and a numbered list.

The simplest way to create these is, again, to ensure that the text cursor is in the correct paragraph (or you have selected a number of paragraphs) and just click on the appropriate toolbar icon (Figure 9.5).

These are again toggles, so that if you have selected a bullet list and you click on the bullet list icon again, you will remove the formatting.

However, if you have a bulleted list and you click on the numbered list icon, you will convert the list to a numbered list (and vice versa). Then, if you click on the numbered list icon again, you will remove the list formatting all together. Note that you do not have to increment the numbers in a numbered list (or, indeed, even type them); this is done for you.

- → This·is·a·bulleted·list¶
- → This·is·a·bulleted·list¶
- → This·is·a·bulleted·list¶
- → This·is·a·bulleted·list¶

¶

1. → This·is·a·numbered·list¶
2. → This·is·a·numbered·list¶
3. → This·is·a·numbered·list¶
4. → This·is·a·numbered·list¶

—

Figure 9.4 A bulleted list and a numbered list.

Figure 9.5 The toolbar list icons.

You can also do all sorts of other things with list formats, for example changing the bullet character and the indent, by going to the **Format** menu and selecting **Bullets and Numbering**. However, this is outside the scope of the ECDL syllabus.

Exercise 9.4

Open the latest version of your test document and add a numbered and a bulleted list. It is a good idea only to use numbers when they actually mean something, e.g. a series of steps. Otherwise, it is simpler to use bullets. However, add an extra paragraph in the middle of your numbered list and see what happens to the numbers of the following paragraphs. Save the version you are happy with.

9.5. Borders

You can apply borders to almost anything within your document. The simplest is to apply a border (or box) to a paragraph. You simply select the paragraph (or paragraphs) you want included, go to the **Outside border** icon (see top left of Figure 9.6) on the toolbar and click. You can change the border you will select (and what is shown initially on the icon) by clicking the arrow to the right to open the box as shown (see Figure 9.6). If you click on a particular style, you will not only apply that style to the current paragraph or to a group of paragraphs selected, but also change the rule on the main icon. Note that if you select a bottom rule, for example, and you have a number of paragraphs selected, the rule will only appear below the last paragraph. If you want a rule after each paragraph, you will have to treat each one separately.

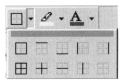

Figure 9.6 Adding a border or box.

Note that if you click a rule style a second time, you will reverse the style change, but if you click another rule style, that will be added or removed, depending on what is currently shown. Thus, if you click a box rule and then click the left-hand side rule, you will end up with a box rule without its left-hand side. Note that you can remove all the rules by clicking the last style shown (all broken lines), which does not toggle. You can vary the style of border and add borders more selectively by using the Borders and Shading format window. Go to the **Format** menu and select **Borders and Shading**. The window (Figure 9.7) will appear. On the left, you will see that you can change the style of the border, its width and the colour. Note that this can also be done from the **Tables and Borders** toolbar (Figure 9.8). We shall come back to Tables in Chapter 15.

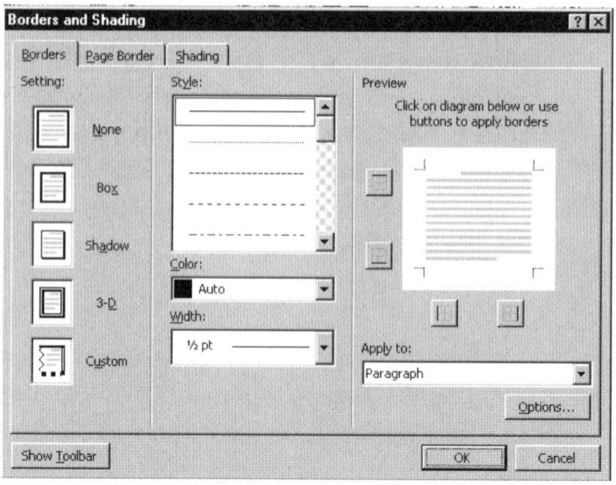

Figure 9.7 The Borders and Shading window.

Figure 9.8 The Tables and Borders toolbar.

If before you open the window, you select some text, then the drop down menu at the bottom right allows you to apply the border to either the whole paragraph or to the selected text. In this way, you can apply underlines, overlines and boxes to individual words or phrases.

Selecting the page border tab brings up a window like Figure 9.9. Here you can opt for a page border similar to those above, as well as determining its position.

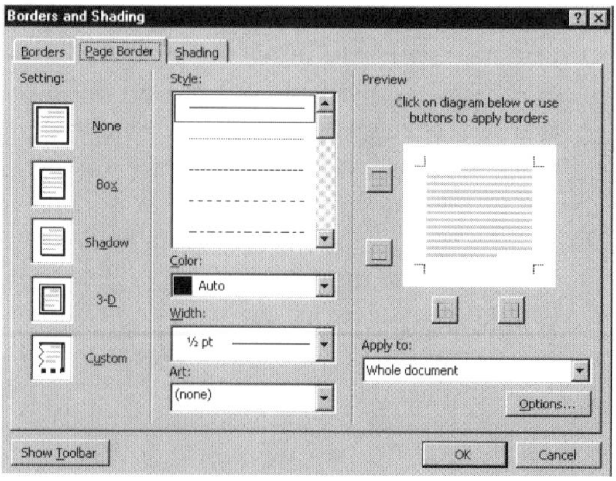

Figure 9.9 Page Border tab in the Border and Shading window.

★ ★ ★
★ ECDL ★
★ ★ ★

Most desktop laser printers do not print to the edge of the paper. There is a narrow strip around the edge of the print area on which it is impossible to print anything. Thus, if you want to include page borders in your documents, you need to experiment with your printer to see what it will print and what it will not.

The final tab in the Borders and Shading format window is, of course, Shading, which allows you to add backgrounds. This is outside the ECDL syllabus.

Facilities such as borders should be used with restraint. Have a look at some printed books to give you ideas about when such features enhance the text and when they are unnecessary.

Exercise 9.5

Open the latest version of your test document. Add a border to a paragraph by using the toolbar. Remove part of it (you can always use Undo). Select a word or a few words in the text and then go to the **Borders and Shading** menu and add a border to the selection. For example, you could enter a telephone number below your address; then select this and add a border to it. You can also add a border to the page and experiment with varying the thickness and type of the rule being used as a border. (Remember to change it back, however, unless you want to keep the new settings.)

Summary

In this chapter:

● We have looked at the use of tabs and tab stops.
● We have looked at using numbered and bulleted lists.
● We have seen how to add borders to paragraphs, selected text and pages.

10

Styles
and Templates

In this chapter you will learn how to

- *Use styles.*
- *Use templates.*

10.1. Introduction

In the last few chapters, we have been talking about applying formats to paragraphs and explaining that the styles applied, the alignment and tab settings used etc., only apply to the current paragraph or any selected paragraphs. It is probably obvious that applying these formats over and over again to different paragraphs would not only take a great deal of time, but would also not take advantage of the storage and processing capabilities of the computer. Thus, just as we can store documents, we can also store and use combinations of formatting, which are called paragraph styles (or usually just styles) and combinations of these styles and other aspects of a document such as the page size etc. (which we will cover in Chapter 13). These combinations are called document templates (or just templates) and we encountered them briefly in Chapter 4.

The ECDL syllabus does not cover the questions of setting up and changing styles and templates, simply choosing and using them. In Chapter 4, we have already mentioned saving documents as templates.

10.2. Using Templates

We shall consider templates first because we can then look at styles within the context of a particular template.

There are two ways you can use a particular template for a document. One is when you create a new document (as we shall see below), while in the other case you may not realise that this is actually what you are doing. This is when you save a document under a new name and delete or change parts of it, so as to use the styles and formats in that document. The document you have used as a pattern may well have a specific template associated with it. This will include a list of styles, as we shall see below, and will also determine the page size, margins etc.

In fact, every document has a template associated with it. In Chapter 2 when we created a new document, we said that you should select a template, which in that case was the blank page. This associates the default template, called normal.dot, with the document; all templates have an extension .dot, as we saw in Chapter 4. In that chapter we also noted that when we saved a file for use on the Web, the page layout changed. This was because a new template, more appropriate for the Web, was then associated with the document.

Exercise 10.2a

Let us go back to creating a new document. Go to the **File** menu and select **New**. In Figure 10.1 you will see that there are a number of tabs along the top of the window and we have selected **Memo**. We select **Professional Memo.dot** and open a new document that looks like Figure 10.2. We have chosen **Memo** because it is relatively simple and the professional one because it is important to be professional!

Figure 10.1 Selecting a template for a new document.

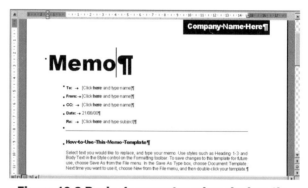

Figure 10.2 Basic document produced when the Professional Memo template is selected.

You will notice that Microsoft has included some text for you to overwrite. This not only tells you what goes where and what to do, but also gives you an idea what the final document will look like. It is not necessary for a template to include text (and, of course, the blank page by definition does not), but it can be helpful. If we had chosen a different template, then the page would, of course, have looked quite different, but we might not have found that out until we started applying the styles. Indeed, even here, although the text refers to the heading styles, you cannot immediately see from the document what those styles will look like. We shall carry on with this in the next section.

We have already mentioned (in Chapter 4) saving documents as templates. Any document can be saved as a template (with or without text), but it is a good idea only to save as templates those files that are indeed different from existing templates or those that have a specific purpose.

Exercise 10.2b

So let's create a new document and choose a template. Since your previous test document was a letter, we suggest that you choose a letter template. You can either follow the instructions in the template or you can try opening the latest version of your test document and cutting and pasting paragraphs from that letter into your new letter (use the **Window** menu to switch between the two documents). You could select the whole of your test document (use Ctrl+A) and the copy and paste it at the end of the new document. You will then need to move parts to the right place (with Cut and Paste). Whichever approach you use, you may find that the style does not change to the new style (in fact it probably will not, because copying and pasting normally carries the style with it – the instances of when it does and when it does not are rather too complicated to detail here). Do not worry, because we shall sort that out in the next exercise.

10.3. Using Styles

It should by now be clear that styles are combinations of formatting instructions (we shall see exactly what very soon) that can be applied to a paragraph. So how can you see and apply these styles? If you go to the **Format** menu and select **Style**, you will open a window that looks like Figure 10.3. We are not going to do anything in this window, but you will see a list of styles on the left, together on the right with previews of the layout and the text style, as well as a description of the style settings of the style selected. The latter may start with **Normal+** or something similar. This means that the style is based on the Normal style, except for the listed changes. Here we are still looking at the **Professional Memo**.

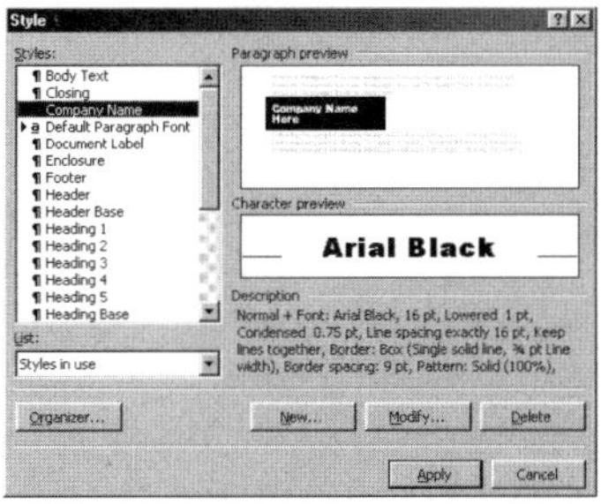

Figure 10.3 The Style Format window.

We said that we were not going to do anything in this window, but, clicking on a different style in the list will show the details for that style instead. The other buttons allow you to change the style and, in many cases, duplicate the operations that we have discussed in previous chapters, but applying them to the style, rather than to a specific paragraph.

We have already looked at the boxes on the toolbar where you can set the typeface and typesize. To the left of these is another box, in which the style name of the current paragraph is shown. It may, for example, say 'Normal' or 'Heading 1'. If you click on the **down arrow** on the right of the box, you will be able to see (or scroll down) the available styles, as shown in Figure 10.4. This duplicates the list in Figure 10.3, but in the correct typeface, at the correct type size and with the size and the text alignment indicated.

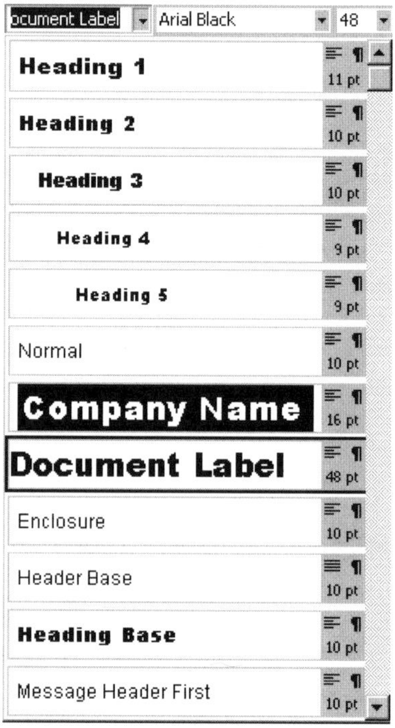

Figure 10.4 The Style drop-down box.

To apply a style to a paragraph, you simply click in the drop-down list and you will see your current paragraph, or any selected paragraph, change to the new style. You can, of course, make direct changes to the formatting of individual paragraphs, but applying the style

★ ECDL ★

elsewhere will not take those changes into account. If you want to make overall changes to a style, you need either to learn how to edit a style or get someone who does understand to provide you with a new template. These are outside the ECDL syllabus.

information

On the Format menu, there is also an option labelled **Style Gallery. This allows you to review the templates and styles on your system and also, to a certain extent, see how your current document would look in a different template. Another option on the Format menu is Autoformat, which effectively analyses your document and applies styles appropriately. Again, this is really beyond the scope of the ECDL syllabus and needs to be used with great care or you may find that changes that you did not intend have been made to your document.**

Exercise 10.3

1. Open the **Style Format** window for your new document (see previous exercise) and click various styles in the list in turn; you should see the details for each style as it is selected. Just click **Cancel** when you have finished looking at the window.

2. Look again at your new document. If you have moved or copied paragraphs to where you want them, you can now apply the appropriate styles by using the drop-down box from the toolbar. Save your new file as, say, *letter01.doc*.

Summary

In this chapter:

● We have looked at the use of templates.
● We have seen how to use an existing template for a new document.
● We have seen that styles are combinations of formats and we have seen how to apply them to paragraphs.

Page Numbering, Headers and Footers

11

In this chapter you will learn how to

- *Add page numbers.*
- *Set up and use page headers and footers.*

●●●●●●●●●●●●⓫●●●●●●●●●

11.1. Introduction

It is almost certainly unnecessary to explain why page numbering is useful. Equally, you are probably familiar with page headers and footers, which may contain the page number, but also include information about a book title and chapter or section title and, in reports, perhaps the name of the organisation, a reference code and the date of the revision.

Of course, you could enter these as part of the text on each page. However that would not be a good idea, because if you change the formatting or the text, your page breaks may no longer be in the required place. In addition, if you add your own headers and footers, they form part of the text and upset the text flow, stopping paragraphs running on from one page to the next.

Fortunately Word provides special routines to handle the inclusion of this aspect of a book or report (as indeed do all top-level word-processing and page make-up programs).

11.2. Adding Page Numbers

You can add page numbers (or folios, as they are known in publishing) to pages without setting up headers and footers as such.

Exercise 11.2

Go to the **Insert** menu and select **Page Numbers**, which will open the window shown in Figure 11.1a. You will see that you can choose where on the page the number is to go and how it should be aligned. The top box gives you the options of selecting the top or bottom of the page, while the alignment box includes the options of **Left**, **Center** and **Right** as well as **Inside** and **Outside** to cater for left- and right-hand pages. You can also choose whether or not to include the page number on the first page.

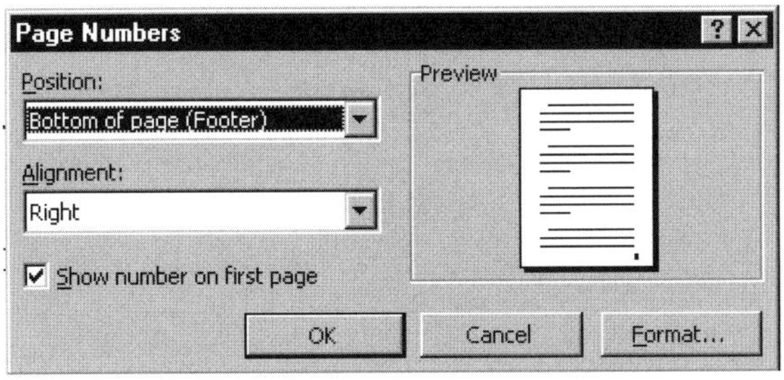

Figure 11.1a The Page Number window.

If you click **Format**, you will open the window shown in Figure 11.1b. Most of the options are self-explanatory, except perhaps the reference to section numbers. Although outside the ECDL syllabus, you need to know that a document can be divided into sections (and, indeed, has to be if you mix, for example, portrait and landscape pages). Here you have the option to restart the numbering of each section (which is another reason for dividing the document into sections) or running it on.

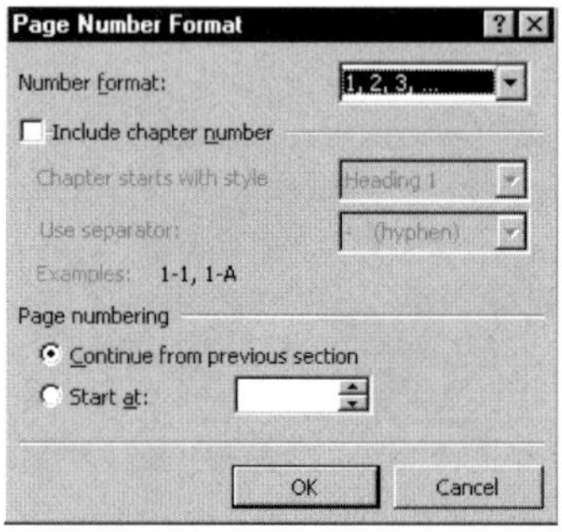

Figure 11.1b Page Number formatting window.

Page numbers only show in Page Layout view and, when you insert them, you will find that Word automatically switches to this view. You can of course switch back. You will also see that the page number is 'greyed' out. If you want to edit it (and there is no real reason why you should, unless you are perhaps unhappy with the typesize), you have to treat it as a footer. You double click on it, which will bring up a window/toolbar that we will discuss below. Note that the page number may appear as {PAGE}, because it is what Word calls a field and it depends on how your system is set up whether field codes are shown or not. You can change this in **Tools I Options I View**. Incidentally, to be sure that you see the actual page number you can use **Print Preview**, which we shall look at in Chapter 14.

You may also notice that three new styles have been added to your drop-down list, Header, Footer and Page Number. These are applied automatically and you would not normally use them in any other context. However, if you know how to do so, they can be changed just like any other style. This is outside the scope of ECDL.

Open your letter file. Add text to ensure that it at least runs on to two pages. Then insert page numbers. Try the different options (you can only insert page numbers in one place, so changing the options will move them, rather than add yet another folio). Again, it may be worth looking at letters from large organisations to see which styles are clear and which are not. Save your file again as a new file or a new version.

11.3. Headers and Footers

Strictly speaking, headers and footers (otherwise referred to as headlines and footlines or running heads and running feet) are present all the time, although you are not aware of them. This is why, if you want to add them, you have to go to the **View** menu, rather than the **Insert** or **Format** menu.

Exercise 11.3a

When you select **Header and Footer** in the **View** menu, you will see three (or perhaps four) things happen:

● If you were not using the Page Layout view, Word automatically switches to this view. In fact, headers and footers are only visible in this view.

● The main page text is greyed out.

● The header area appears.

● A new window, effectively a toolbar, appears.

These effects are all shown in Figure 11.2. If you mouse over each of the icons on the toolbar, you will see an explanation of what each means. On the left, you will see **Insert AutoText**, which is shown with its drop-down menu displayed. The entries are in general self-explanatory; AutoText entries can be edited and added by going to the Tools menu, choosing **AutoCorrect** and then the **AutoText** tab. Use of it is outside the ECDL syllabus, but some aspects are useful in the context we are discussing here. The insertion takes place at the position of the text cursor.

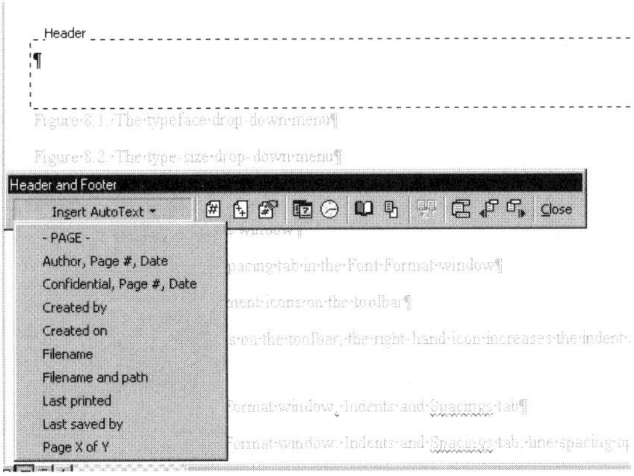

Figure 11.2 Viewing headers and footers with AutoText displayed.

The remaining icons then fall into groups:

● Two of the next three icons effectively duplicate the page number commands we looked at above, while the third allows you to insert the total number of pages.

● The next two icons allow you to insert date and time. Note that these can also be used by going to the **Insert** menu and choosing **field**, where you will see many other fields; all of these can, of course, be inserted anywhere in a document.

● The next icon allows you to access **Page Setup**, which we will discuss in Chapter 13. The other icon in this group allows you to hide or show the main text while you are editing the header and footer. This has no effect on the file itself.

● The next icon, in a group of its own, allows you to make the header the same as the previous one, that is, the same as the header in the previous section. If there is no previous section, it will be 'greyed' out.

● The first icon of the last group, before **Close**, allows you to move between header and footer, while the other two icons in this group allow you to move between sections.

The implication of some of these icons is that different sections can have different headers and footers, although they do not have to be different, and this is indeed the case. Having different headers and footers is often a good reason for splitting a document into a number of sections. For example, the 'Prelims' of a book (title page, table of contents, preface, etc.) are often numbered with Roman numerals and the main book pagination is in Arabic numerals.

If you click **Close**, you return to the view you were in before you opened the headers and footers.

Other than the above, you handle text in headers and footers just as you would other text. You can apply any style to text in a header or footer and can also use all the usual formatting options.

You should note that headers and footers expand if the contents becomes greater than the original size (and headers and footers can contain pictures as well as text), so you need to handle them with care. Note also that the position of the header and footer is set in the **Page Setup** (Chapter 13).

★ ECDL ★

caution!

It is a good idea either simply to insert a page number or to use headers and footers if you want a more complex layout. While you can use both in the same document, it is not advisable, because it can lead to confusion. In general, use simple page numbering when that is all you need. Use headers and footers when the situation is more complex. Remember that you cannot see either in the Normal view!

Exercise 11.3b

Open the version of your letter file in which you included page numbers and add headers and footers to see what happens. If you include a page number field in the header or footer as well as inserting a page number, you will end up with two folios, which is generally not a good idea. Do not save this file.

Exercise 11.3c

Open the version of your letter file without page numbers and add an appropriate header and/or footer. Save this as a different version/file from the version in which you simply added page numbers.

Summary

In this chapter:

● We have looked at inserting page numbers (folios).
● We have looked as adding headers and footers to a document.

Checking and Changing Spelling and Grammar

12

In this chapter you will learn how to

- *Use a spell-check program and make any necessary changes.*

- *Use a grammar-checking program and make any necessary changes.*

★ ECDL ★

12.1. Introduction

Word provides facilities that check your spelling and your grammar. The first thing you need to be sure of is whether Word is talking the same language as you are. To do this go to the **Tools** menu and select **Language** and then **Set Language**. The language that is already set for your document will be highlighted. You can change this if you wish.

Note that there are various versions of English; UK English assumes that you want to spell words with -ise, -ising, ised and -isation at the end, rather than using -ize etc. This means that you have to be careful if you want to use British spelling for words such as colour, but the -ize option as well (which some publishers such as Oxford University Press recommend). While you can set up customised dictionaries, this is outside the scope of ECDL. It is not documented whether the grammar checking also has variations between the different versions of English.

12.2. Checking and Correcting Spelling

In earlier versions of Word, you had to run the spell checker to see if Word thought you had made any errors. You still can, either by pressing function key F7 or by going to the **Tools** menu and selecting **Spelling and Grammar**. Note that by going to **Tools** I **Options** I **Spelling and Grammar** you can specify whether not you check the grammar at the same time (and you can also change this in the window that is displayed when a potential error is found, Figure 12.1). If you have some text selected, the check will only take place on the selected text.

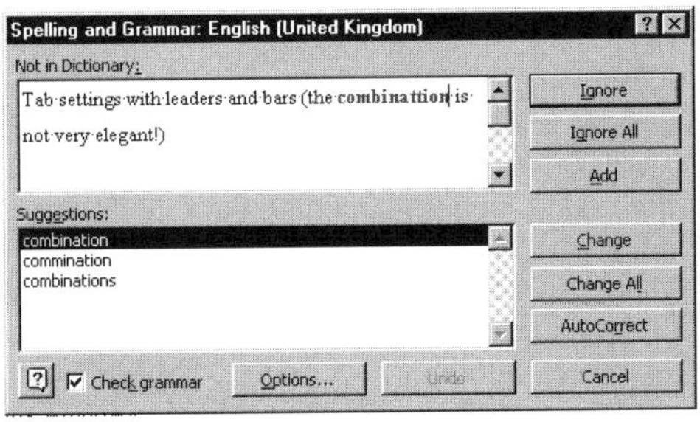

Figure 12.1 A possible spelling error is found.

If the spell check hits a word that it thinks is wrongly spelled, then you will see a window like that in Figure 12.1. You can choose from the following options:

● **Ignore or Resume**: Go on to the next word; make no change.

● **Ignore All**: Go on to the next word; do not make any change and do not query this word again if it occurs in the document.

● **Add**: Add to your custom dictionary. You can also edit this dictionary by going to **Tools | Options | Spelling and Grammar** and pressing the **Dictionaries** button.

● **Change**: Change to the suggestion highlighted in the **Suggestions** box. You can select the right word if it is there. If it is not and you still need to make a change, then you can overtype in the box at the top. If your new word is also not in the dictionary, then you will see another message and have to decide whether to ignore the word or add it to your custom dictionary. You can also choose **Ignore All**, which will allow you to use the highlighted word in the present document, but not add it to the dictionary.

● **Change All**: Change all occurrences of the word in the same way.

● **AutoCorrect**: This will make the correction and add it to the list of words that are automatically corrected as you type. Be careful about using this option in the spelling check, because you may find that you add changes that are wrong! Fortunately, you can access and edit the **AutoCorrect** list, via **Tools | AutoCorrect**.

Note that the **Options** button takes you directly to **Tools | Options | Spelling and Grammar**, while there is also a tick box that allows you to decide whether to check grammar or not, as we noted above.

Word 97 makes life easier for you, however, in that, if you have indicated so in the **Options** menu, all words that Word thinks are wrongly spelled will have a wavy red underline. To view alternative spellings, right click on the word (see Figure 12.2). To leave the word unchanged, just click away from the pop-up menu (although it will retain the underline). Alternatively, you can click on **Ignore All**, when the underline will disappear. Thus, to see which words may be 'wrongly' spelled, you just need to scan the document by eye.

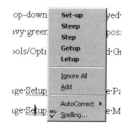

Figure 12.2 Drop-down window displayed after word with wavy red underline is right-clicked.

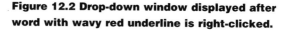

caution!

It is worth remembering that all a spell checker is doing is comparing the words you use with a dictionary. It may not be correct from your point of view and will make some odd, and sometimes amusing, suggestions for proper names. Furthermore, it will not find words misused, e.g. principle instead of principal, effect instead of affect, so spell checking needs to be used intelligently and with caution. Nevertheless, spell checkers are extremely useful utilities if used properly.

Exercise 12.2

Open your letter file. If you have made any potential spelling errors, they will, by default, already be underlined with a wavy red line. Right click on these and decide what to do. You can also go to the **Tools** menu and select **Spelling and Grammar** (or just key F7). At present, uncheck the **Check grammar** box and work through the document. If you wish, you can introduce deliberate spelling errors or proper names to see what happens. Save your corrected document.

12.3. Checking and Correcting Grammar

The grammar checker works in exactly the same way as the spelling checker as far as the interface is concerned. Indeed, you cannot run the grammar checker independently of the spelling checker, except in so far as that grammatical errors are underlined with a wavy green line, rather than a red one, so right clicking on an example will bring up the possible grammar error (see Figure 12.3).

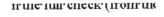

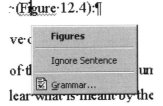

Figure 12.3 Drop-down menu displayed after phrase or sentence with wavy green underline is right-clicked.

If you use **Tools | Spelling and Grammar** the options that you have are similar to those with the spell checker, but fewer (see Figure 12.4):

115

● **Ignore or Resume**: Make no change and move on.
● **Ignore all**: Make no change to any instance of this error in the document and move on. Do not highlight this error again. It is not entirely clear what is meant by the same error.
● **Next sentence**: Move on within the passage shown.
● **Change**: Change as suggested or as you rekey.

Spelling and Grammar: English (United Kingdom)	? X
Comma Use:	
You still can either by pressing function key F7 or by going to the Tools menu and selecting Spelling and Grammar.	Ignore / Ignore All / Next Sentence
Suggestions:	
can	Change
Check grammar Options... Undo	Close

Figure 12.4 Possible grammar error is found.

Note that in the **Tools | Options | Spelling and Grammar** menu (Figure 12.5) Word allows you to select various writing styles and to even generate your own style, but only by selecting from the list of Settings provided.

Options	? X
Track Changes / User Information / Compatibility / File Locations	
View / General / Edit / Print / Save / Spelling & Grammar	
Spelling	
☑ Check spelling as you type	
☐ Hide spelling errors in this document	
☑ Always suggest corrections	
☐ Suggest from main dictionary only	
☑ Ignore words in UPPERCASE	
☑ Ignore words with numbers	
☑ Ignore Internet and file addresses	
Custom dictionary: CUSTOM.DIC	Dictionaries...
Grammar	
☑ Check grammar as you type	
☐ Hide grammatical errors in this document	
☑ Check grammar with spelling	
☐ Show readability statistics	
Writing style: Standard	Settings...
Casual / Standard / Formal / Technical / Custom	
Check Document	OK Close

Figure 12.5 The option to choose writing styles in the Tools | Options | Spelling and Grammar window.

★ ECDL ★

If care is needed in using a spelling checker, then even more care is needed in using a grammar checker. It can certainly be useful in throwing up obvious errors, such as double spaces, misplaced punctuation etc., but it often suggests unnecessary changes (for example, the Word grammar checker does not like passive clauses) and is even sometimes wrong. For example, it can sometimes wrongly recommend singular or plural verbs. So, use the grammar checker, but use it intelligently!

In Section 2.3 we noted the spelling and grammar status icon. If you double click this icon, you will move to the next grammar or spelling error.

Exercise 12.3

Open your letter file. If you have made any potential grammar errors, they will already be underlined with a wavy green line. Right click on these and decide what to do; you may well disagree with the advice given! You can also go to the **Tools** menu and select **Spelling and Grammar** (or just key F7). This time, check the **Check grammar** box and work through the document. You will almost certainly find something that the grammar checker does not like. You will also see any spellings that you left uncorrected in the last exercise. Save your corrected document.

Summary

In this chapter:

- We have looked at using a spelling checker.
- We have looked at using a grammar checker.

Document Set-up

- *Use page set-up.*
- *Change page size, page orientation and margins.*

ECDL

13.1. Introduction

We have looked at formatting paragraphs and imposing styles, but so far we have not mentioned how to define the overall layout of the document, page size, paper size and so on. These are all defined and modified by using Page Setup, which is on the File menu.

13.2. Paper Size and Paper Source

When you open **Page Setup**, the first tab you see is usually margins. However, we will look first at **Paper Size** and **Paper Source** (Figures 13.1a and 13.1b).

Exercise 13.2a

In **Paper Size**, you set the size of the paper that you (or more correctly your printer) will be using. Note that versions of Word when installed may have the default paper size set to the US standard letter (8.5 by 11 inches). You can set the paper size to **A4**, which is what most people in the UK use, but you should also click on the **Default** button to change the default paper size. You will be asked whether you want to do this. You should click **Yes**, but it is a good idea only to make this change of paper size at this time, so that all other settings will be retained.

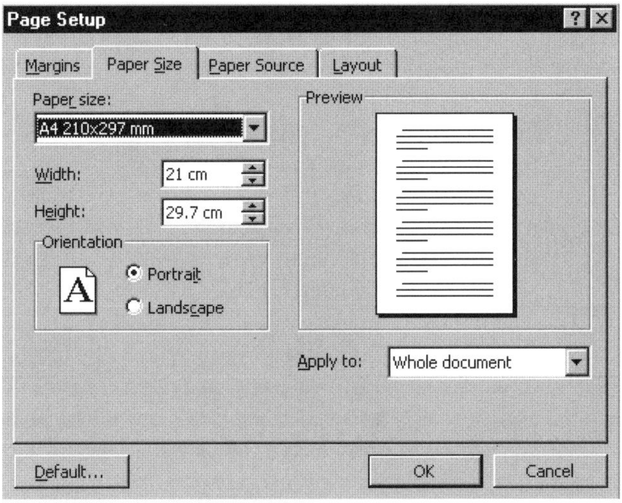

Figure 13.1a Paper Size tab of Page Setup window.

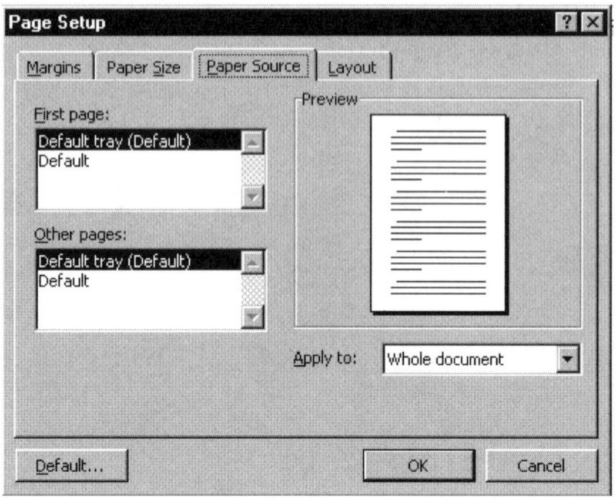

Figure 13.1b Paper Source tab of Page Setup window.

In this menu you also set whether your document is to be portrait (long side vertical) or landscape (long side horizontal). Note that you can apply these settings to the whole document or just from this point on. If you have sections in the document, you can apply the change just to one section (useful if you want one section to be landscape and the rest portrait). Note that you see a preview.

What is shown in **Paper Source** will depend on the printer you have set up on your system. Note that you have the option to take paper for the first page from one tray and the paper for the remaining pages from another tray. This is to cater for letters where the first page and the continuation pages often use different notepaper. It depends on what you are doing (and whether your printer allows this) as to whether this facility is useful to you. And, of course, if you have a printer that will take more than one size of paper, you can set up sections to go on different paper sizes.

Exercise 13.2b

Open your letter file, which will almost certainly be portrait, although the paper size may be US standard letter. Open the **Page Setup** window from the **File** menu. Change the size to **A4**, which is almost certainly the size of paper you will be using if you are in the UK or any other part of Europe. It is probably a good idea to change the default as well. See what happens if you change the page orientation to landscape, although you will probably not want to leave your letter like this. **Save** the document if you have changed the page size. You can look at the **Paper Source** tab, but you are unlikely to want to change anything here, unless you are on a network, in which case talk to your network manager.

13.3. Margins

The first four entries (see Figure 13.2a) are self-explanatory and indicate the distance from the edge of the paper to the edge of the text area. They are shown in the preview.

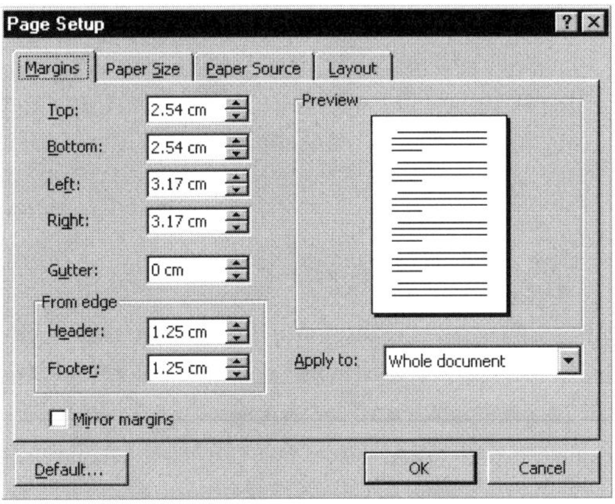

Figure 13.2a Margins tab of Page Setup window.

The next box, **Gutter**, needs some explanation. It refers to what is also called a binding margin. It will be added to the left-hand margin. However, if you have the **Mirror margins** box ticked it will be added to the right-hand side of left-hand (verso) pages and to the left-hand side of right-hand (recto) pages, as the preview shows. (Note that you may have to click on the **Apply to** box to change the preview.) Figure 13.2b shows the effect on the page preview. Mirroring the margins of course also reverses the margin settings on the left-hand page.

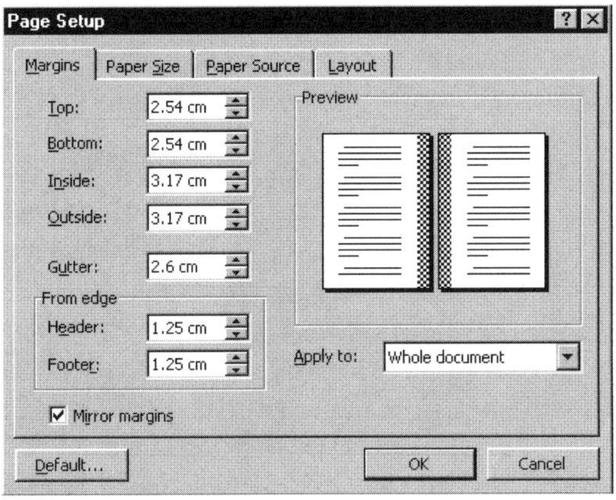

Figure 13.2b Margins tab with Mirror margins set and a gutter added.

The other two boxes determine the positions of the top of the header and the bottom of the footer in terms of the distance from the top and bottom of the page respectively.

You can also change the left and right margins of a page by dragging the page markers on the ruler. Note that you usually need to select the whole document or you will only change the margins for the paragraphs selected. If you do the same thing in Print Preview (Chapter 14), you can move all the margins, both horizontal and vertical. This is equivalent to changing them in Page Setup.

caution!

Remember that most printers do not print right up to the edge of the paper, so you need to make sure that you do not site your header and footer too near to the edge of the page. The same, of course, applies to left and right margins, but aesthetic and filing considerations usually make this unlikely anyway.

The last tab in the **Page Setup** window is **Layout** (Figure 13.3). Again this is quite self-explanatory and mainly to do with sections and headers and footers. It also allows you to specify line numbering if you wish. This was also referred to in the **Paragraph Format** window in Chapter 8.

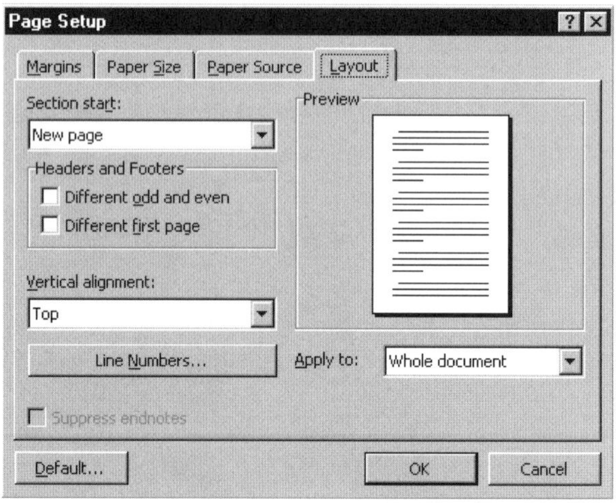

Figure 13.3 The Layout tab of the Page Setup window.

★ ★ ★
★   ★
★ ECDL ★
★   ★
★ ★

●●●●●●●●●●●●●⑬●●●●●●

Exercise 13.3

1. Open the latest version of your letter. Try changing the margins and, if you included a header and footer, the distance from the edge of the page. Set what you think may be reasonable. Add a binding margin if you wish. Are you planning to print the second page on the back of the first? If so, then set **Mirror margins**. You can also experiment with having different odd and even headers in this case by using the **Layout** tab. Again, once you are happy, save the latest version.

2. Ideally, the format that you now have should be one you would like to use for a real letter. You can therefore, if you wish save this as a template, calling it perhaps *Myletter.dot*. It is probably a good idea to delete all the text except your address (and telephone number). Note that you can always edit this later if you wish.

Summary

In this chapter:

● We have looked at how to use Page Setup.
● We have seen how to change the page size and orientation.
● We have seen how to set the default page size.
● We have seen how to change the paper source if necessary.
● We have seen how to modify and mirror the page margins and the positions of the header and footer.
● We have seen how to add a gutter or binding margin.
● We have seen how to add line numbers.

14

Printing Documents

In this chapter you will learn how to

- *Preview a document.*
- *Use the basic print options.*
- *Print a document from an installed printer.*

★ ECDL ★

●●●●●●●●●●●●●●●⑭●●●●●

14.1. Introduction

Even in this age of electronic communication, it is more than likely that you will need a printed version of a file you have been working on. Windows is able to store details of many printers and you can switch between them if they are attached to your system. However, there is always a default printer, which is the one to which documents are sent unless you indicate otherwise.

Although the printers are installed from Windows itself, all control of the printing of documents is done from within Word. And not only can you print from within the program, but you can also preview what you are going to print. As we saw in Chapter 11, the Page Layout view may not give you a true WYSIWYG (What You See Is What You Get) view, whereas the Print Preview does.

14.2. Print Preview

To see a print preview of your document, as mentioned in Chapter 13, go to the **File** menu and select **Print Preview**. There are various tools shown on the special toolbar (see Figure 14.1):

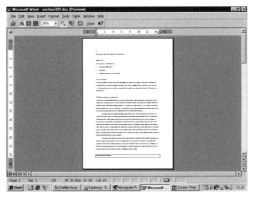

Figure 14.1 The Print Preview window.

● You can print directly from this preview.
● You can select the magnifying glass and zoom in and out by simply clicking on the page.
● You can show a single page or up to six pages at the same time.
● You can choose the exact magnification that you want to use.
● You can display both horizontal and vertical rulers if you wish. These allow you to modify the margins, as discussed in Chapter 13.
● You can shrink the view to fit.
● You can use a full-screen view, so that the menu bar disappears.

When you exit from Print Preview, you return to the document view you had previously. You do not close the file. If you print directly from Print Preview, you open the Print dialogue box, as we shall see below.

Exercise 14.2

Open the latest version of your letter file and then open the **Print Preview** from the **File** menu. **Zoom** in and out and vary the magnification. Change the number of pages you can view. Show the rulers and experiment with the margins (if you do this, either use **Undo** or, better, make sure that you do not save the new version of your file). Try some of the other options. Do not at this stage print. You can close the **Print Preview** and even the file, if you wish, when you have finished.

14.3. Using Basic Printing Options, Including Choosing the Printer

To print a file, you can print from the Print Preview, you can select the toolbar icon 🖨 , you can select **Print** from the **File** menu or you can use the keyboard shortcut (Ctrl+P). Whichever option you choose, when you decide to print, you will see the menu shown in Figure 14.2.

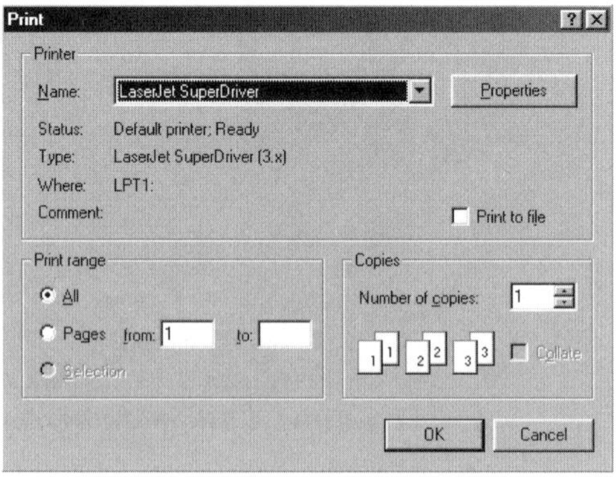

Figure 14.2 The Print window.

You can therefore choose which printer to use (the one that is shown initially is the default printer and you will only see the printers that are installed), which pages to print, how many copies to print (and how to collate them). You can also determine whether you print the document itself or certain related information, but this is not within the ECDL syllabus. You can also print just odd or just even pages, as well as all pages in the range you have set.

If you click on **Properties**, you see another window (Figure 14.3), which varies depending on the printer; since each printer has its own driver software that determines what you see here. What always appears, however, is the option to change the paper size since, as has already been mentioned, you may find that many applications use the US letter size as default. You will probably need to change this to A4; this is a separate setting from that in **Page Setup**, which sets the page size for the document rather than the printer and the orientation of the page on the printer, portrait or landscape. Once you have made your selection, click **OK** and then again **OK** in the main printer window.

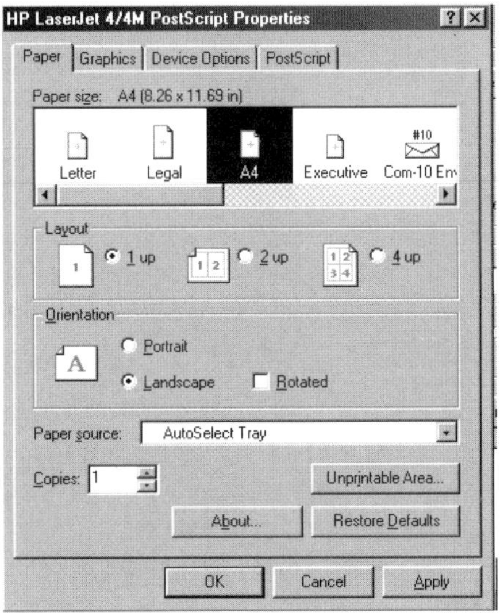

Figure 14.3 The Print Properties window.

Exercise 14.3

Open your final letter document and, by whatever method you prefer, print it onto your default printer (or another one if you prefer). Are you happy with what you get? If not, then you may need to go back and change some of the things you set in previous exercises.

14.4. Viewing the Progress of Printing

If you have sent a number of documents to be printed, you may wish to review their progress. This actually forms part of Module 2, but is repeated here because it is information that you may find very useful in the word processing context. You can do this from the desktop print manager. There are two ways to do this.

Exercise 14.4a

step **1.** Open the **Printers** window from the Start menu (**Start | Settings | Printers**) and then select the printer you are currently using and open it. You will see a window like that in Figure 14.4, which shows you the progress of the various print jobs you have sent to this printer.

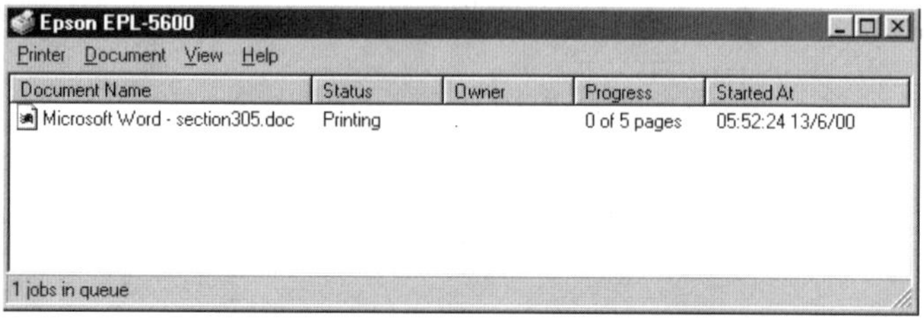

Epson EPL-5600				
Printer Document View Help				
Document Name	Status	Owner	Progress	Started At
Microsoft Word - section305.doc	Printing		0 of 5 pages	05:52:24 13/6/00

1 jobs in queue

Figure 14.4 Progress of print jobs.

step **2.** When you start to print, you will see a printer icon open in the **Taskbar** at the bottom right of your screen (next to the time in most cases). If you click on this, you will see the same window as in Figure 14.4. The icon will remain as long as there are files being printed. When printing is complete, it will disappear.

information

> **From the print manager screen, you can also pause or purge printing. This can be useful if, for example, you have a long print queue and suddenly have something urgent to print or if the printer jams and you need to stop printing.**

Exercise 14.4b

Try printing several documents and then open the **Print Manager** window. Relate what is happening there to what is coming out of the printer. Note that sometimes, because a printer may take some time to process the page internally, it may be even a few minutes after a print job has disappeared from the Print Manager window before it is actually printed.

Summary

In this chapter:

- We have looked at how to use Print Preview.
- We have looked at how to set the print parameters and the printer properties.
- We have looked at how to monitor the progress of printing.

Creating, Editing and Formatting Tables

- *Set up a table in various ways.*
- *Edit and format a table.*

15.1. Introduction

In Chapter 9 we looked at the use of tab stops and noted that their use was good for short items, but for blocks of text, for example, this was not a good approach, because tabs only handle text on a line by line basis. Tables in Word, however, are based on a cellular approach, so that a table is essentially a block of cells, to each of which separate formatting can be applied. You can also apply formatting to the whole table or on either a column or a row basis.

15.2. Creating a Table

There are two ways you can create a table by using commands (Section 15.6 explains how to draw a table):

Exercise 15.2

● Use the icon ▦ on the **Standard** toolbar, which opens a grid (Figure 15.1) on which you can choose up to five columns by four rows by default. However if you drag and drop with the right mouse button, starting in the top left cell, you make the table any size you like. Figure 15.2 shows a table of four columns and three rows produced in this way. (Note that if you select text before you click the icon, you will convert that text into a table with the number columns corresponding to the number of tabs you have set in the paragraph, although the result is not always easy to predict.)

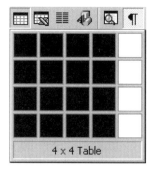

Figure 15.1 Table options shown when using toolbar option.

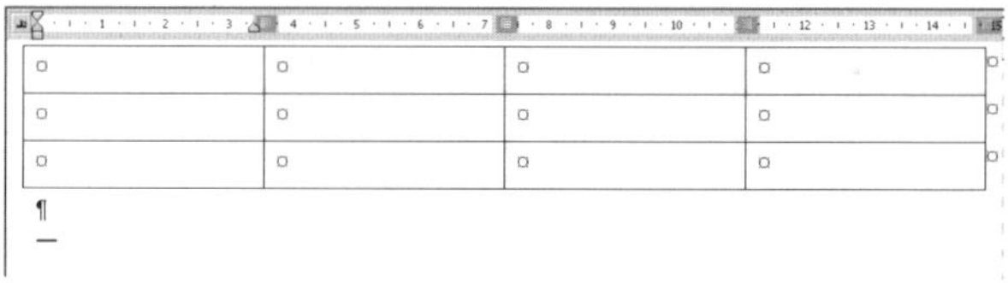

Figure 15.2 Example of table created with toolbar option.

★ ECDL ★

● Go to the **Table** menu (tables have their own menu) and select **Insert Table**. You then see the window shown in Figure 15.3. You can choose the number of columns and rows, as well as the column widths if you wish, although **Auto** is a good first choice (and is what the icon approach generates automatically), providing equal widths with the total table width equal to the page width. If you make your columns wider, some of the table may be off the edge of the page!

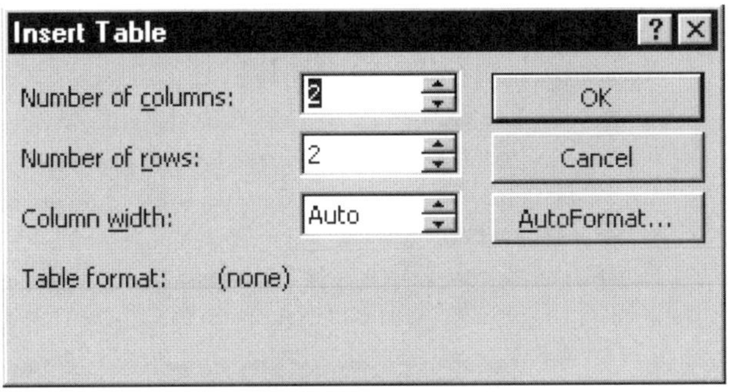

Insert Table		? ✕
Number of columns:	2	OK
Number of rows:	2	Cancel
Column width:	Auto	AutoFormat...
Table format:	(none)	

Figure 15.3 The Insert Table window.

Note that with the second approach, you can at the same time select **AutoFormat**, which we shall look at below. The other point to note is that, unless you use **AutoFormat**, which you can also select from the **Table** menu, each cell of the table will initially take on the format of the paragraph in which you create the table. Thus if we choose another table of four columns and three rows, it will appear below the first table, as shown in Figure 15.4. You will note that the two tables are identical.

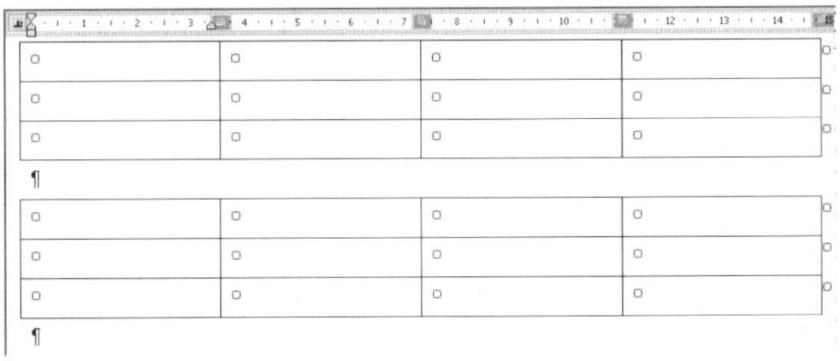

Figure 15.4 Tables created via menu and toolbar options.

Now create a new file (with a blank page template). Try creating a table by either of the above approaches. See which you find easier. For use in a future section, create seven columns and head the columns as follows: *Title, Firstname, Surname, Address 1, Town, County and Postcode.* Enter some text in those columns corresponding to the column headings. Create at least five rows in addition to the heading row. It does not matter whether you use real names and addresses or not. Save the file as *table_test01.doc*.

15.3. Changing Cell Attributes

The first thing to note is that there are various selections you can make in a table:

Exercise 15.3a

step **1.** You can select a row, again using **Select Row** from the **Table** menu or using the mouse. When you do the latter, make sure that you include the column marker for the end of the row, which looks as though it is outside the table (Figure 15.5(a)). If you do not do this (see Figure 15.5(b)), you will have selected the cells making up the row and not the row itself.

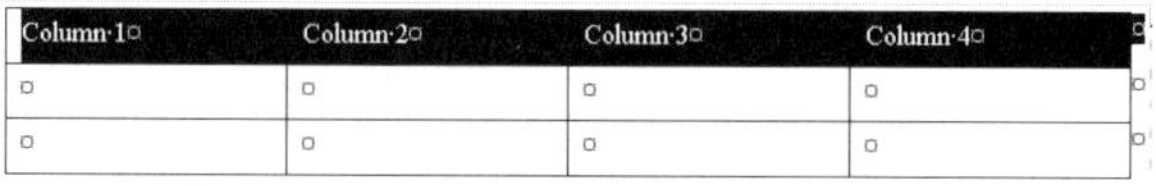

Column·1▫	Column·2▫	Column·3▫	Column·4▫	▫
▫	▫	▫	▫	▫
▫	▫	▫	▫	▫

Figure 15.5a A row selected.

Column·1▫	Column·2▫	Column·3▫	Column·4▫	▫
▫	▫	▫	▫	▫
▫	▫	▫	▫	▫

Figure 15.5b Cells in a row selected.

step **2.** You can select a column, again using **Select Column** from the **Table** menu, by using the mouse or by moving your mouse cursor down to the top of the column. In the latter case it will change into a broad arrow and the column will be selected if you then click (Figure 15.6).

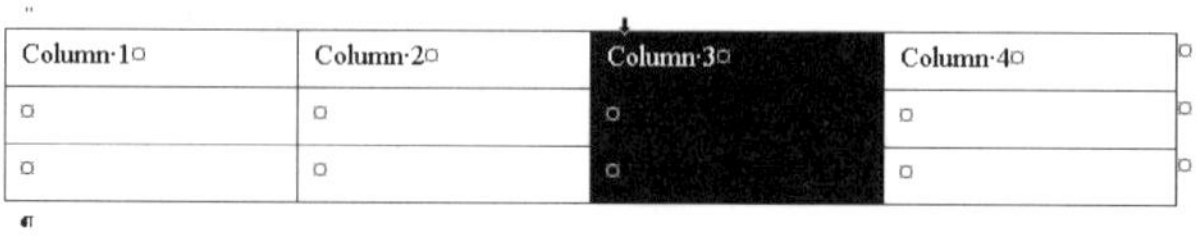

Column·1▫	Column·2▫	Column·3▫	Column·4▫	▫
▫	▫	▫	▫	▫
▫	▫	▫	▫	▫

Figure 15.6 Selecting a column.

step **3.** You can select the whole table, using **Select Table** in the **Table** menu or using the mouse in the usual way. Again, it is important to make sure that you include the last column marker.

step **4.** You can select a cell or cells with the mouse.

Once you have made this selection, you are able to do different things:

● If you have selected a row, then you can format or delete (all the cells in) that row. To delete, you use **Delete Row** from the **Table** menu; if you just use the delete key, you will end up with an empty row, i.e. you delete the contents but not the row. You can also insert a row, but you do not have to select the row to do that, just place the cursor in the row below where you want to insert the new row and click on **Insert Row** from the **Table** menu. However, if you select a number of rows, when you select **Insert Row** from the **Table** menu you will insert the same number of rows as you have selected. Thus if you want to insert three rows, you select three rows below where you want to insert the new rows and then select **Insert Row**.

● If you have selected a column, then you can again format (all the cells in) that column. To delete, you use **Delete Column** from the **Table** menu; again do not use the Delete key. As with rows, if you select two columns and then choose **Insert Column** from the **Table** menu, you will insert two rows to the left of the rows you had selected. Even to insert one column, you need to select a column; if you do not the **Insert Column** command will not appear in the **Table** menu (to replace **Insert Row**) – the same is true of **Delete Column**. Note that to add columns to the right of the table, you select the column formed by the markers on the right of the table and then choose **Insert Column**.

● If you select the whole table, you can, of course, delete the whole table (use **Delete Row** again) or you can format the whole table. You can also convert the table to text (with or without tab stops) or sort entries in it. These two aspects are really outside the ECDL syllabus, but are useful techniques. Note that by selecting text and going to the **Table** menu, you can also convert the text to a table, which can be very convenient. This is a more controllable approach than selecting the text and using the **Insert Table** icon.

● If you select a cell, you can format this, as well as deleting the cell, inserting additional cells and moving the cell boundaries (as we shall see shortly). However, once you do any of the last three operations, you will find that the table is much more difficult to handle. This is because the columns, and perhaps also the rows, will cease to align and making changes in terms of the rows and columns, which is great advantage of handling information as tables, is much more unpredictable. What you can do, however, is merge cells, so that you are able to produce cells that straddle either vertically or horizontally or alternatively split a cell into a number of other cells (Figure 15.7).

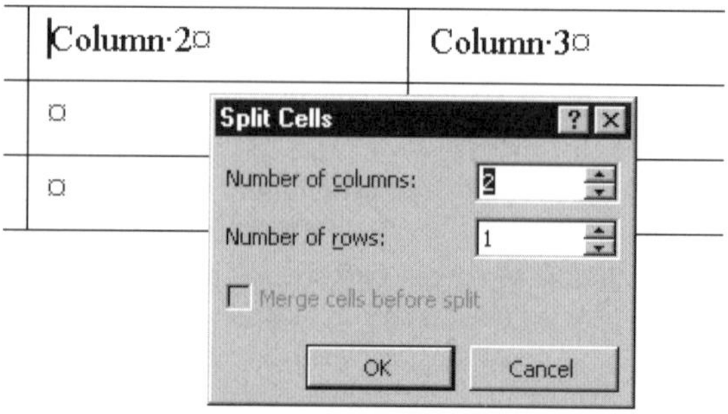

Column·2¤	Column·3¤
¤	
¤	

Split Cells   ? X

Number of columns: 2

Number of rows: 1

☐ Merge cells before split

OK   Cancel

Figure 15.7 Splitting a cell.

caution!

In Word 6, the predecessor of Word 97, when you selected two columns in a table and then chose Merge Cells, the two columns were merged cell by cell, so that two columns became one. Unfortunately, in Word 97, merging two columns gives one enormous cell, which is not very helpful. There are ways around this, but they involve various tricks. So if you have a specific requirement to merge columns, for example to make three columns containing honorific (Mr, Mrs, Ms etc.), first name and surname into a single column containing the full name with honorific, then see if you can obtain a copy of Word 6 to run on your system alongside Word 97!

information

If you want to add a row at the end of a table, the easiest way is to click in the last cell of the table (placing the text cursor in that cell). Then press the tab key and the text cursor will move to the next cell, thus creating a new row in the process. This is an illustration of the role that the tab key plays in tables. It does not insert a tab character as such. It moves the cursor from cell to cell starting at the top left and going along the rows until it reaches the bottom right. Holding down the Shift key while pressing the tab key moves the cursor in the opposite direction. If you want to key a tab character within a table cell, for example to align a column on the decimal point, then you have to key Ctrl+Tab.

ECDL

You can change column widths with the mouse. If you move the cursor to one of the grid lines indicating a column boundary, it will change into a double vertical line with an arrow on each side (see Figure 15.8). If you now drag and drop the cursor, the column boundary will move to a new position.

Note that, as pointed out above, if no cells are selected, then the whole column boundary moves, while if one (or both) of the cells adjacent to the boundary is selected, only the boundary of that cell or those cells will move. In either case, it is simply the boundary that moves, so if one column becomes wider, the adjacent column becomes narrower. Getting column widths correct can therefore be an iterative operation.

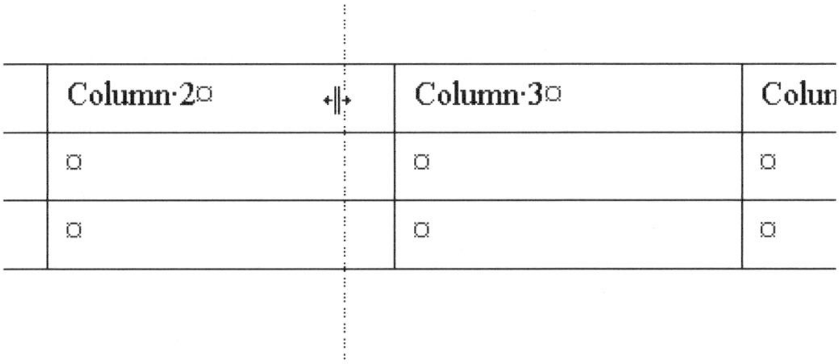

Column·2◻	┽‖┾	Column·3◻	Colun
◻		◻	◻
◻		◻	◻

Figure 15.8 Moving a column boundary.

You can also change the column width, as well as the row height, by using **Cell Height and Width** from the **Table** menu. This is the only way to adjust cell height and, if you know the width of the information that you want to put into the cells, perhaps a better way of adjusting the width as well.

Exercise 15.3b

First you select the cells to be modified. Whether you select a complete column or a complete row is unimportant as the formatting will apply anyway to the complete row or column. Then choose **Cell Height and Width**. Unless you select a column, you will first see the Row tab (Figure 15.9). This has various boxes you can complete:

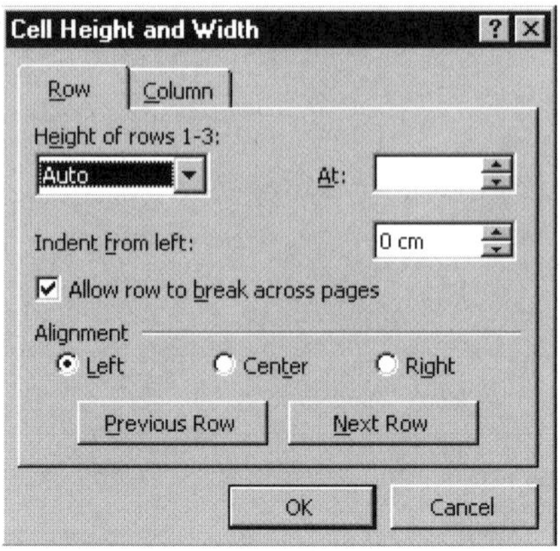

Figure 15.9 Row tab in Cell Height and Width window.

● **Height of rows**: It is a good idea to set this at **Auto** or at **At least** (with the value in the box on the right). While you can set it exactly, you may find entries disappearing because either the typesize is too large for the height or the text goes onto two rows, for example.

● **Indent from left**: Remember this applies to the whole row and not the text.

● **Allow row to break across pages**: This is a question of style and personal preference.

● **Alignment (Left, Center, Right)**: Again remember that this applies to the whole row.

You can then go on to sort out the next row or group of rows. A group can, of course, be the whole table. Note that there is also a command on the **Table** menu, **Distribute Rows Evenly**. However, the actual row spacing is not completely under your control if you use this. The rows are averaged over the table depth.

If, in the **Cell and Height** menu, we move to the **Column** tab (Figure 15.10), we see that we have two options to complete, plus **AutoFit**:

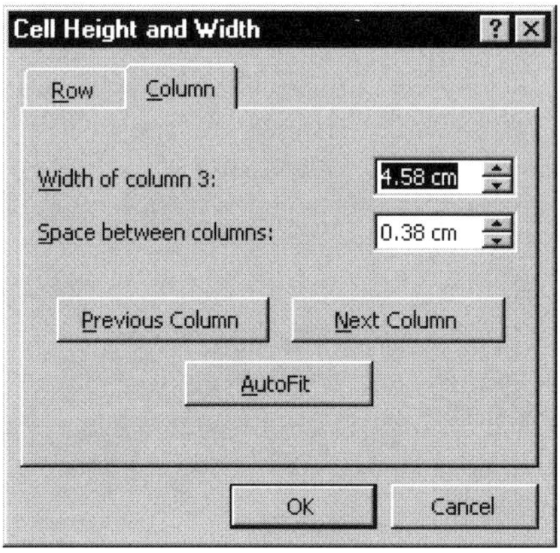

Figure 15.10 Column tab in Cell Height and Width window.

● **Width of columns**: This can obviously be set at any value, but again be careful that the aggregate width does not exceed the page width.

● **Space between columns**: This can be varied at will. If you have rules between the columns, this value can often be set narrower than the default, which seems to be quite wide.

● **AutoFit**: Here the columns adjust to the width of the contents in so far as they can within the page width.

Again there is a command on the **Table** menu, **Distribute Columns Evenly**. This distributes the columns within the width of the table.

So now open your table file. Try inserting columns, rows and even cells, to see what the effect is. Delete columns, rows and cells. Once you are happy with carrying out the operations, close the document and do not save it.

Open your table file again. Change column widths and row heights and even the type size in columns and rows until you feel that the table is as readable as you can get it. Then save it as a new file or a new version.

15.4. Formatting and AutoFormat

As noted above, you can format table cells as you wish, using all the formatting facilities used in normal text. It is also quite possible to have special table cell styles in a template. However, to make life easier for you Microsoft has developed a series of standard formats.

Exercise 15.4

These are accessed by selecting **AutoFormat**, either when creating the table or from the **Table** menu. The **Autoformat** window (Figure 15.11) now appears. The box at the top left lists the formats; if you select them in turn, you can see what each one looks like in the **Preview**. Lower down the window, you can select the aspects (borders etc.) you wish to use, as well as deciding what to do about the first and last row and/or column, which may be a heading or a total, for example. If you click **OK**, your table will take on the formatting that you have selected.

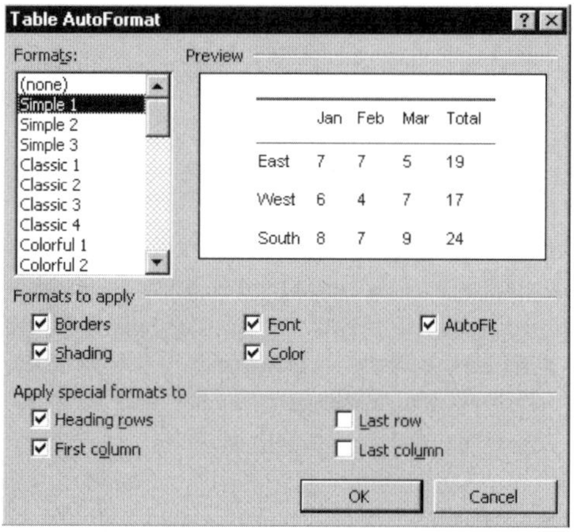

Figure 15.11 The Table AutoFormat window.

There is one final aspect of cell formatting and this can only be done from the **Tables and Borders** toolbar (Figure 15.12), which you can open from **View | Toolbars**, from the icon ▦ on the main toolbar. This is aligning the text at the top, in the centre and at the bottom of a cell. To do this you select the relevant cell(s) and click on the preferred icon from one of the following: ▤▤▤

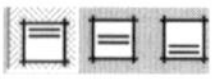

Figure 15.12 The Tables and Borders toolbar.

So, open your first table file again. Use **AutoFormat** to see if you can achieve a better effect than you did in the last exercise. Save the file again as a new file or a new version.

15.5. Splitting a table

If you click in any row of a table and then select **Split Table** from the **Table** menu, the table will split above the row in which you clicked, creating a blank line, i.e. a carriage return, between what are now two tables.

Exercise 15.5

Open your first table file again. See what happens when you split the file. Do not save it.

15.6. Drawing a Table

Word also allows you to draw a table. To create a table, you do the following:

Exercise 15.6

1. Either click on the pencil at the left of the **Tables and Borders** toolbar or choose **Draw Table** from the **Table** menu. Your (mouse) cursor will turn into a pencil and the toolbar will open if it is not already showing. The view will change to **Page Layout**.

2. Click where the top left corner of the table is to go.

3. Drag and drop until the overall size of the table is about right (Figure 15.13).

Figure 15.13 Drawing the outside of a table.

4. Click at the top of the box you have created, roughly where you think the boundary between the first two columns should be, and draw a line to the bottom of the box (Figure 15.14).

Figure 15.14 Indicating the first column boundary of the table.

5. Repeat this for as many columns as you want.

6. Click on the side of the box or on a column boundary for the position of the first row and draw a line across the box, straddling as many columns as necessary.

7. Again, repeat for as many rows as you want (Figure 15.15).

Figure 15.15 Indicating the last row boundary when drawing a table.

8. Click again on the **Pencil** icon or strike the Esc key on the keyboard to exit from drawing mode.

You can then tidy up your table and add formatting in the ways we have discussed above.

Now open a new file. Create the same table as you did in the first exercise, but this time by drawing. See which approach you prefer. You can save this file if you wish, but do not overwrite your last previous table file.

15.7. Adding Borders and Shading

Word offers a number of different ways to achieve borders and shading for your table, as we shall now see.

●●●●●●●●●●●●●●●●●⑮●●●

Exercise 15.7

To add borders, you can either use the **Tables and Borders** toolbar (Figure 15.12) or the normal boxing tool bar that we have used previously in Chapter 9 (which is in fact the same as the one on the **Tables and Borders** toolbar since icons can be on more than one toolbar). You simply select the appropriate cell(s), row(s) or column(s) (or even the whole table) and then choose the rules you want to add. It is a good idea to use **Print Preview** to check that the rules are where you want them. The grid lines in a table are very useful but they can be confusing. You can hide them if you wish (see the **Table** menu).

To change the weight and type of rule you are using for the border, you can either use the icons on the **Tables and Borders** toolbar again or you can use the **Borders and Shading** option from the **Format** menu, which we covered in Chapter 9. Similarly, you can change the colours of the rules and the fill (or shading) of a table cell. If you use the toolbar, you just click on the pencil icon ✎ for the rules or the paint can icon 🎨 for the fill and choose what you want from the selection now displayed (Figure 15.16). Remember, however, that you may also need to change the colour of your font (see Chapter 8) if your text is to be visible.

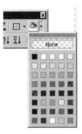

Figure 15.16 The fill selection on the Tables and Borders toolbar.

So finally, open your latest formatted table file again (not the one where you used **AutoFormat**). Add some rules and perhaps some shading. How does it look in comparison with the AutoFormatted table? Save if you wish.

Summary

In this chapter we have looked at:

● Three different ways of adding tables to a document.
● How to select cells, columns, rows and complete tables.
● Reformatting and deleting cells, columns and rows.
● Splitting cells and splitting a table.
● Adding borders and shading to table cells.

16

Drawing Objects and Handling Images

In this chapter you will learn how to

- *Add an image or graphics file to a document.*
- *Use AutoShapes and rules.*
- *Change the colours of drawn objects.*
- *Move images and drawn objects.*
- *Resize and crop a graphic.*

16.1. Introduction

Many documents contain illustrations. From a technical point of view there are two kinds, those known as bitmaps and those known as vector graphics. Bitmaps are images, often digital photographs, made up of many small dots, known as pixels, either black and white or coloured (Figure 16.1). Vector graphics, in contrast, are based on a combination of lines and shapes that can be described mathematically (Figure 16.12) and redrawn each time they are shown on screen or sent for printing.

Figure 16.1 A bitmap image.

Figure 16.2 A drawing or vector graphic.

In some ways the two types of artwork are handled similarly, while in others they are treated quite differently, so it helps if you understand the difference. One important factor, for example, is that the file size of a piece of vector artwork is almost independent of the size at which it is output and in fact, the same illustration can be reproduced at any size because it is scalable. In contrast, a bitmap is created at a fixed resolution, i.e. with a fixed number of dots (pixels) per unit length in each direction. Put simply, each dot contains the information about the colour at that point and over its own small area. If you enlarge a bitmap, you may be able to create more dots, but you cannot increase the information content; thus the quality of the picture gradually gets worse and the impression of continuous tone cannot be sustained. To obtain a larger bitmap at the same resolution, you need more dots with each dot containing its own information. Another effect of this is that the larger a bitmap is, the larger its file size is.

Strictly speaking, these differences are not part of the ECDL syllabus, but they will help you understand why the two types of artwork are handled differently. Indeed, you will find that there are different types of program for handling the two types, although there is some overlap. More important, understanding the difference will help you to use artwork more sensibly. For example, a letter containing a photograph will have a large file size, so that it will take a long time to print and will take longer, and therefore cost more, to transmit electronically, quite apart from taking up more space on your system.

There are ways to compress files so that their file size is smaller, but these methods do not affect the time taken to print. These compression techniques are also not as appropriate for files used for printing as they are for files viewed on screen. You will see more about images for viewing on screen in Module 7, but here we will restrict ourselves to looking at how to add them to documents, how to generate some kinds of drawings and how to move and resize the illustrations.

16.2. Adding an Illustration

There are essentially two ways in which you can include a picture in your document; you can draw it yourself or you can bring it in (import it) from somewhere else, in just the same way as you would have done had you been generating a paper based document in the old-fashioned way. And again, just as in the old way, even if you draw the picture, you may choose not do it directly within the document, but complete the drawing somewhere else and insert the finished drawing into your document.

If you add either a bitmap image or a drawing to a Word document, the techniques you use are the same, because you are simply including another file within your document file. While it is useful to understand the differences between the two types for practical reasons, importing a file is importing a file. In fact, we shall see more about importing other types of file in Chapter 17.

You can either add an illustration directly in the text of your document or, together with some additional text, you can put in a text box, which is a box that is separate from the main flow of the document text and can be moved independently. The use of text boxes is outside the ECDL syllabus, but it is a good idea to understand the principle. Here we shall just discuss inserting illustrations directly in the text.

Exercise 16.2a

If you want to include an illustration, you decide where it should go, placing your text cursor at that position. Then you go to the **Insert** menu and choose **Picture**. Here we will be concerned with the top two entries in the menu you now see (Figure 16.3) **Clip Art** and **From File**. In fact, they only distinguish the source of the image and the method of inclusion.

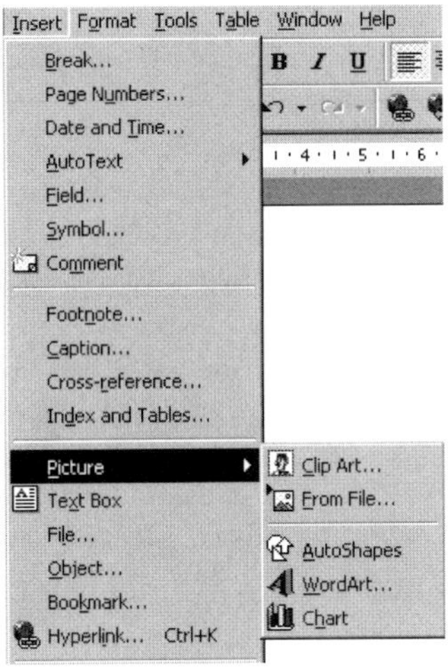

Figure 16.3 The Insert Picture menu.

If you select **Clip Art**, you open up Microsoft's **Clip Art Library** (Figure 16.4). You will also see that the view changes to **Page layout**. In order to take advantage of the whole library, you will probably need to have the Microsoft Office CD in your CD drive, but this depends on how your system is set up. You will almost certainly have a selection of pictures on your hard disk (and you may see a series of information screens before you see the window like Figure 16.4 if you do not have the CD in its drive).

You will see that the images are in categories, but to begin with you see All Categories. If you choose, say, **Transportation**, you will see a window like Figure 16.5. In the full library there are a large number (several thousand) pictures, so using the search facility provided may help find what you want. Figure 16.6 shows the search screen. Note that, although you want a picture, you have to search for it by the keyword or name that has been given it, so it may be worth remembering that the names were given in the USA.

Figure 16.4 The Microsoft Clip Art library.

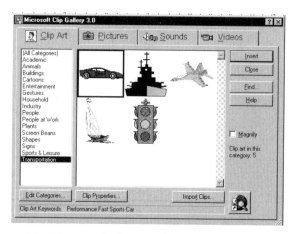

Figure 16.5 Transportation section of the Clip Art library.

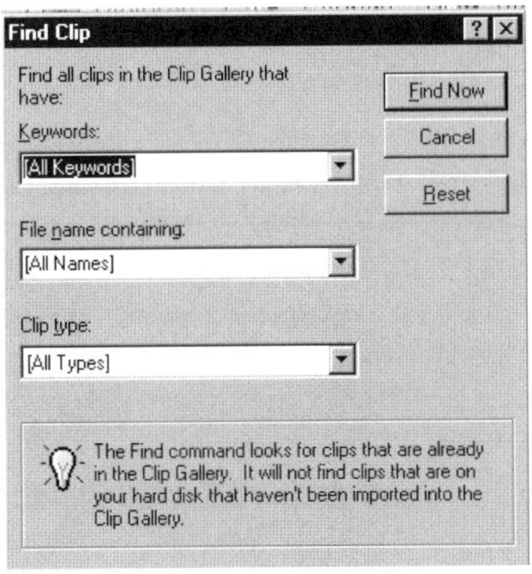

Figure 16.6 Search window of the Microsoft Clip Art library.

Once you have found the image you want, you select it and click on the **Insert** button and the picture will be inserted into your original document.

caution!

One of the problems with Word is that the exact position of the picture is not always predictable, although as we shall see below, you can specify the rules for placing picture. Do not be surprised initially, if the picture does not appear where you expect it to. The position depends partly on the size of the picture and partly on your page size and where the callout was on the page. However, once it is part of your document, you can move it around.

Once you have inserted the picture, the Clip Art Gallery closes and, if you want to insert another picture, you have to reopen it. This can be a little tedious if you want more than one picture, but there seems to be no way to keep the window open. Note that, if you click on **Clip Properties**, you see a window like Figure 16.7, which tells you the path name of the file, as well as its size and file format. Although we shall not consider them here, there are a large number of different graphics and image file formats.

Clip Properties ? ✕

File name: sailboat

File type: Windows Metafiles
File size: 10422 bytes

File path: C:\Program Files\Microsoft Office\Clipart\Popular\sailboat
Previews in: C:\Program Files\Microsoft Office\Clipart\Popular\POP97.

🔒 This preview file is read-only. You cannot modify its properties.

Keywords:

Performance Ship Navigate

Categories:

☐ Academic
☐ Animals
☐ Buildings
☐ Cartoons
☐ Entertainment
☐ Gestures
☐ Household
☐ Industry

OK

Cancel

New Category...

Figure 16.7 The Clip Art Properties window.

If you decide that Microsoft's offerings are not what you want or, alternatively, you have a scanned photograph or one taken on a digital camera that you want to include in the document, then when you choose **Picture** from the **Insert** menu, you choose **From File** instead of **Clip Art**. You will now see a window like Figure 16.8. In fact, you can access the Clip Art library this way as well if you know the folder it is in (which you can take from the screen in Figure 16.7). You will notice that in the box at the bottom left you can specify the file type and conveniently all picture types are grouped together.

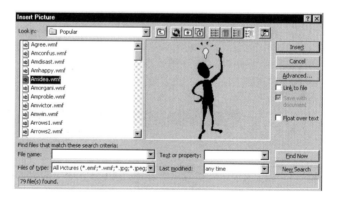

Figure 16.8 The Insert Picture window.

★ ECDL ★

You can again search (either by file name or by text or property) and you can also browse and, as you do so, you will see previews on the right of the window. Once you have the picture you want, you select **Insert**. Note that there are one or two other buttons and options on this screen:

● **Advanced**: This allows you to carry out more complex searches.

● **Link to file**: If this box is ticked, then, rather than the picture being inserted in the file, a link to the picture is added. This has advantages and disadvantages. Of course, it keeps the file size down, but, if the document is passed to someone else, you have to remember to include a copy of the artwork file and update the link (although the next box **Save with document** helps you with this). In addition, when you look at the file on the screen, the picture has to be called in each time you scroll, which can slow down the scrolling.

● **Float over text**: If this box is ticked, then the situation is the same as with the Clip Art Library and the position is unpredictable, being placed in a picture box between paragraphs at the position that 'looks best'. However, this may not be the most appropriate place with reference to your text. Thus removing the tick from this box means that the picture goes exactly in the text at the point where you called it from. This may, of course, mean that it disappears off the edge of the page, but you can always move it (by **Cut** and **Paste**). The problem comes if you edit the document and then have to reposition the picture. However, although the floating option copes with this in principle, you may find that the solution is not always what you want. You will need to find the best solution to your needs. This is not one of Word's better aspects.

Note that Word also provides a **Picture** toolbar (Figure 16.9), but most of the adjustments it allows you to make are not covered in the ECDL syllabus. In addition, whilst the toolbar provides some basic functionality, there are much better tools than Word for handling pictures.

Figure 16.9 The Picture toolbar.

You can, of course, always, copy an illustration from another document and paste it into your document. While this is not the place to discuss it at length, remember that the copyright of almost all illustrations belongs to someone and so their use in any commercial or widely distributed document without permission or payment is infringing the copyright owner's rights.

Exercise 16.2b

1. Open a new file; you will need some text, although it does not matter what it is about; you could copy the text from anywhere – a Help file perhaps. If you prefer, you can open your letter file. Insert the Windows 98 CD in your drive. Go to the **Insert** menu and select **Insert Picture** and then **Clip Art**. If you have opened the letter, see if you can find an appropriate picture to include; otherwise just select any picture you fancy. You could try using **Search**. Once you have found a picture, see what happens when you add it.

2. Go to the **Insert picture** again. This time select **From File**. Do you have any photographs on your system? If so, you could try inserting one. If not, go to the **Microsoft Clip Art Gallery** again, download a photograph off the web or perhaps find another CD that has photographs on it. Use browse (or find) to locate files with an extension such as .jpg, .bmp, .gif, .tif or .pcx. and try the different options in the **Insert Picture** window.

16.3. Adding and Handling AutoShapes

If you want to draw a diagram in a Word document, then there is a facility called **AutoShapes**, which makes things much easier than starting from scratch.

Exercise 16.3

If you look again at Figure 16.3, you will see that **AutoShapes** is an option in the **Insert I Picture** menu. If you select **AutoShapes**, your view will switch to **Page Layout** and you will see the **AutoShapes** toolbar (Figure 16.10a); alternatively, you can open the **Drawing** toolbar (Figure 16.10b) and open **AutoShapes** from there. Mousing over the images shown tells you what they are and if you click on, for example, **Basic Shapes**, you will see the selection shown in Figure 16.10(c). If you then select a shape, your (mouse) cursor will change into a cross and you can drag the image until it is the size and shape you want. Note that, if you keep the Shift key held down while you do this, you retain the aspect ratio; that is, a square remains a square rather than becoming a rectangle. You will see that the **Callouts** are set up to allow you to enter text directly into them (Figure 16.11). You can format the text in the usual way, as described in Chapter 8.

Figure 16.10a The AutoShapes toolbar.

Figure 16.10b The Drawing toolbar.

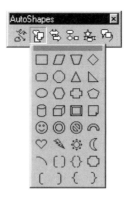

Figure 16.10c AutoShapes toolbar displaying Basic Shapes.

Figure 16.11 A callout.

It is worth noting that simple shapes, such as rules, arrows, squares/rectangles and circles/ellipses can be drawn directly from the Drawing toolbar (Figure 16.10b).

AutoShapes provides you with the basic shapes, but you will probably want to change the line widths and you may also want to change the colour of the lines and the fill. In Figure 16.12, we will look at a simple square. Figure 16.12a shows it as created (and selected). Now, you may have noticed that when you opened the AutoShapes toolbar, you also opened the Drawing

151

toolbar, which allows you to carry out most drawing operations, many of which we shall not consider here. However, if we ensure that our square remains selected (Figure 16.12b shows it when it is not selected and clicking on it selects or deselects it), then we do the following:

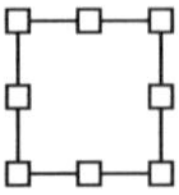

Figure 16.12a Square is created and selected.

Figure 16.12b The square unselected.

step**1.** Select the **Line style** icon ≡ . Clicking on it opens the menu shown in Figure 16.12c. You just choose the line thickness you want; we have chosen 3 pt (3 points). Note that you can also change the dash style and (for certain objects, but not the square) add arrow heads .

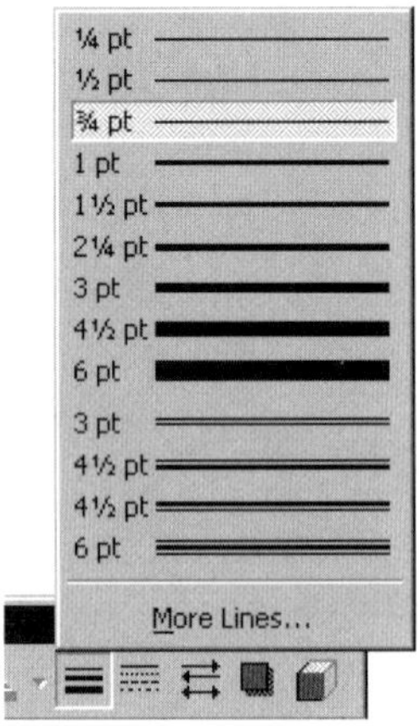

Figure 16.12c

step**2.** Next you may want to change the colour. Click on the **Line colour** icon and select what you want (Figure 16.12d). Here we have chosen grey, as this guide is not in colour (Figure 16.12e).

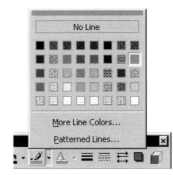

Figure 16.12d The Line colour menu.

Figure 16.12e The square with a grey outline.

3. Finally, you may want to change the fill colour. Click on the **Fill colour** icon and you will see a menu that is very similar to Figure 16.12d. Again choose your colour. In this instance we have chosen black (Figure 16.12f).

Figure 16.12f The square with a grey outline and black fill.

You can also vary these parameters using the **Format AutoShape** menu, which we shall look at in the next section.

Now open a new file or the one in which you added the picture. Experiment with using **AutoShapes** to add shapes to your file. Save the file if you wish.

16.4. Moving and Placing Images and Drawn Objects in a Document

Images can be sited in three ways. They can 'float' between paragraphs, they can be fixed, as we saw above, and they can overlap the text, as do AutoShape objects unless you make space for them or adjust the wrapping.

Exercise 16.4

For AutoShape objects adjusting these parameters is carried on the **Format AutoShape** menu. You access this by right clicking on the edge of the object. A drop-down menu will then appear. Select **Format AutoShape** at the end.

The menu initially looks like Figure 16.13 and you can see that here you can also make the changes we made using the **Drawing** toolbar.

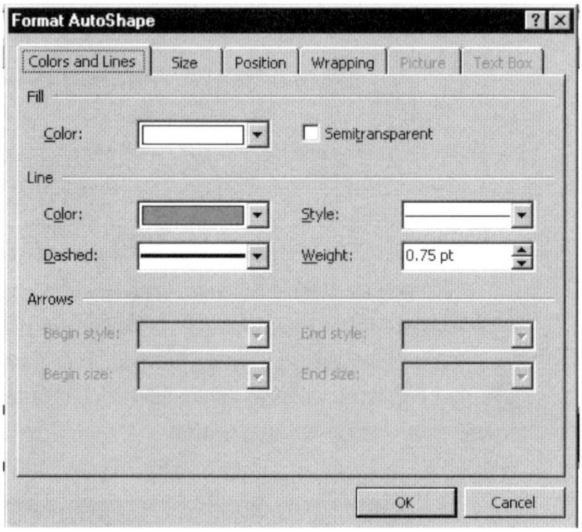

Figure 16.13 The Format AutoShape window.

The other tabs are:

● **Size**, including rotation. (This is not shown here, but is very clear.)

● **Position** (Figure 16.14). You can specify the position both horizontally and vertically relative to the page, the column, the paragraph and the margin. You can also fix the position and allow the image to move with the text. Locking the anchor (and you will see an anchor ⚓ alongside a paragraph when the object is selected) means that the object will always appear on the same page as its 'parent' paragraph. Allowing the image to move with the text means that the image moves with the paragraph as you edit. Note that **Floating** is not an option here.

Figure 16.14 The Position tab.

● **Wrapping** (Figure 16.15). This shows how the text can flow around the object and the pictures on the menu illustrate the principles well. The dark square shows what is currently selected. Initially there is no wrapping so the object may overlap the text.

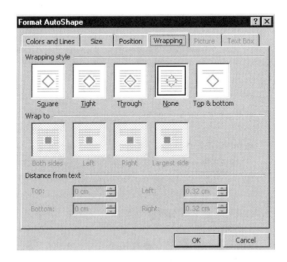

Figure 16.15 The Wrapping tab.

If you want to move a picture, you have some of the same options. Again you right click on the picture and then choose **Format Picture** from the end of the pop-up menu that appears. The **Format Picture** menu is similar to the

Format AutoShape menu, but has some differences. The **Position** tab now allows the picture to float in addition to the other options. You can now also access the **Picture tab** (Figure 16.16), which allows you to crop the image (see below) and make some adjustments to colour, as well as allowing you to treat the image as a watermark, which shows on every page. We shall not deal with that here.

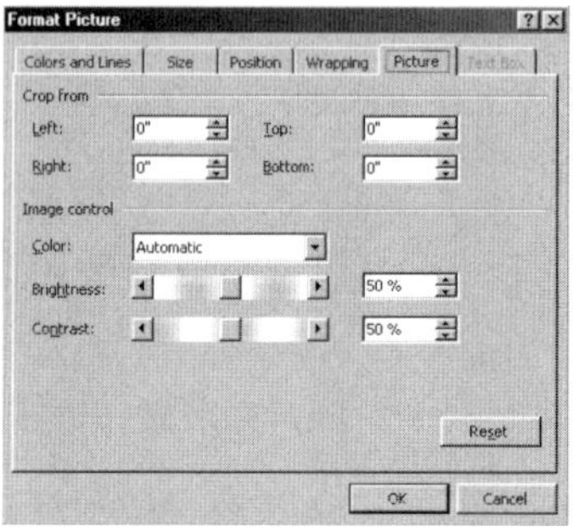

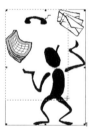

Figure 16.16 The Picture tab of the Format AutoShape window.

The **Picture** toolbar, which we have already seen in Figure 16.9, allows you to make many of the same adjustments.

Use your file with the pictures in. Then experiment with the **Format AutoShape** and **Format Picture** menus or with the **Picture** toolbar to see the ways in which you can place your picture(s) and shapes relative to the text. **Save** the file if you wish.

16.5. Sizing and Cropping Images

To size an image, you simply select the object (picture or AutoShape) and then drag one of the 'handles' (the small boxes on the sides and corners) to the size you want (Figure 16.17). Using one of the handles on the sides will distort the aspect ratio (height to width). If you use a corner handle and hold down Shift, you will retain the aspect ratio.

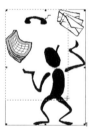 

Figure 16.17 Resizing a picture: (left) during; (right) after.

Cropping a picture means removing part of the picture (as if you were cutting it off). To do this, you either specify the crop in the **Picture** tab or you select the crop tool ⌗ from the **Picture** toolbar. The cursor shape will change to this shape. Then, in the same way as sizing, you drag one of the handles (Figure 16.18). This time, the size will not change. When you have finished, just click in a blank part of the screen to cancel the cropping tool.

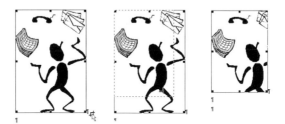

Figure 16.18 Cropping a picture: (a) before; (b) during; (c) after.

Exercise 16.5

1. Resize one or more of your pictures. (You can always use **Undo** or close the file without saving.)

2. Crop one or more of your pictures. (You can always use **Undo** or close the file without saving.)

Summary

In this chapter:

- We have looked at the difference between vector graphics and pictures (bitmaps).
- We have seen different ways of adding an illustration.
- We have noted that the copyright of almost every illustration is owned by someone.
- We have seen how to use AutoShapes.
- We have seen how to move and place images relative to text.
- We have seen how to resize and crop images.

Importing Objects

- *Import spreadsheet files.*
- *Import image files, charts and graphs.*

17.1. Introduction

We have seen in the last chapter how images can be inserted into a document. However, these are not the only objects that can be inserted and the approach used in Chapter 16 is not the only approach possible. One of the advantages of Windows is that you can insert an object, such as a spreadsheet, into a Word file in such a way that when you want to edit it, selecting it also opens the application that is associated with it (often the application that it was created with). How applications are associated with file types is discussed in Module 2. For example, files that have an extension .doc are almost always associated with Word and files with an .xls extension with Excel.

There are a number of ways in which you can transfer text and pictures into Word. The simplest is copying and pasting and this works from many applications. The second approach is to use **Insert** and then select **File**. This only works for file types for which Word has an input filter and these include Excel. The third approach is the one we have mentioned above, using what is called OLE (Object Linking and Embedding) and here you go to the **Insert** menu and select **Object**.

We shall now deal with the three approaches in turn.

17.2. Copying and Pasting

We have looked at copying and pasting in detail in Chapter 6. The approach is just the same here, except that we have to open the other application first. Figure 17.1 shows a small spreadsheet in Excel (see Module 4 for more information on spreadsheets). If we select the cells containing the data and then copy (probably just keying Ctrl+C), the material has been added to the ClipBoard.

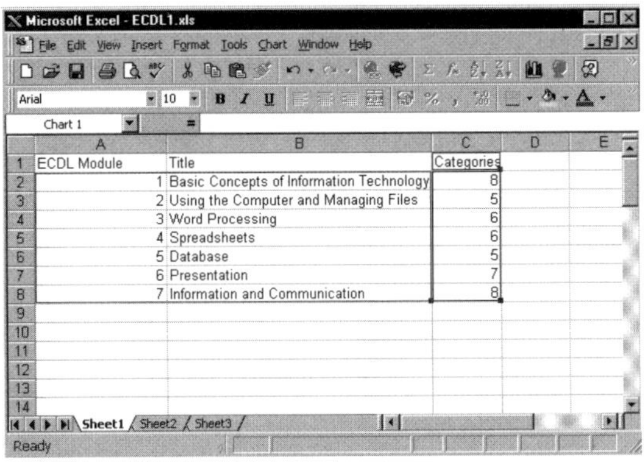

Figure 17.1 A small spreadsheet in Excel.

Next we have to transfer to Word (or open it if it is not already open) and ensure that we have the right target document open. Moving/switching between applications is described in Module 2, but a brief summary is given in Chapter 2 of this book. Once you are in the Word document at the position where you want the table to be inserted, you simply **Paste** (key Ctrl+V). The Excel data will appear as a table (Figure 17.2) that can be edited in the ways discussed in Chapter 15. Note that copying in this way breaks the link with the original application.

ECDL Module	Title	Categories
1	Basic Concepts of Information Technology	8
2	Using the Computer and Managing Files	5
3	Word Processing	6
4	Spreadsheets	6
5	Database	5
6	Presentation	7
7	Information and Communication	8

Figure 17.2 The Excel spreadsheet pasted as a table into Word.

However, there is a way of copying that does not break the link and we will come to that below.

Exercise 17.2

Once you know how to use Excel, create a small file, then create a Word file and try copying the Excel file yourself. You could also try with other applications, such as graphics and drawing programs.

17.3. Inserting a File

The second way to include a file from another application (usually just the Microsoft applications and one or two others such as WordPerfect and Lotus 1-2-3) is to go to the **Insert** menu and select **File**. Assume we have saved our spreadsheet as *ECDL1.xls*, so if we find this to insert, we will see the filter menu (Figure 17.3). (Incidentally, this shows us just which application files we can import.) The imported file (below the one we copied and pasted) can be seen in Figure 17.4 and is almost identical.

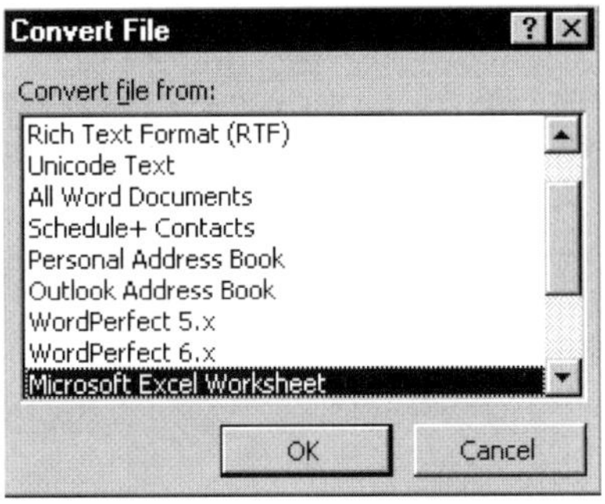

Figure 17.3 Importing a file using the Convert File window.

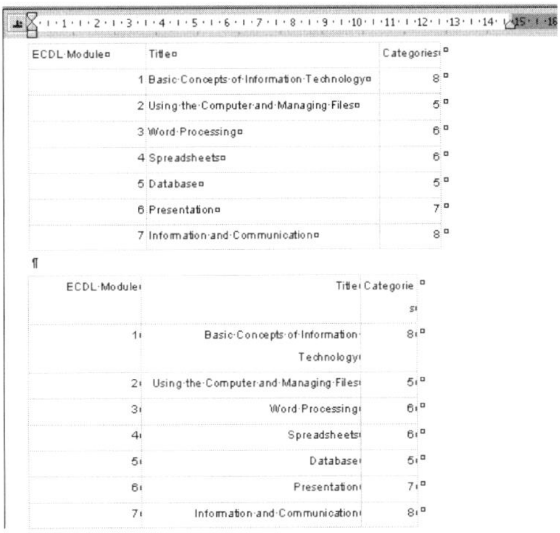

Figure 17.4 The Excel spreadsheet imported into Word.

This approach also breaks the link with the original application. There are advantages in both this method and copy and paste. For the whole file, particularly if it is large, the insert approach is probably better, but you do have to have the whole file. If you only want part, then use copy and paste.

17.4. Inserting Objects

The third approach allows the link we discussed above to be retained.

Exercise 17.4

If you go to the **Insert** menu and select **Object**, you see a window like Figure 17.5a with the tab **Create New**. The list shown includes essentially the software that you have available and if you select, for example,

Microsoft Excel, you open an Excel spreadsheet within your Word document. Although it forms part of the Word document, it is edited with Excel, which provides you with increased functionality. And, of course, you can choose any of the programs that are compatible.

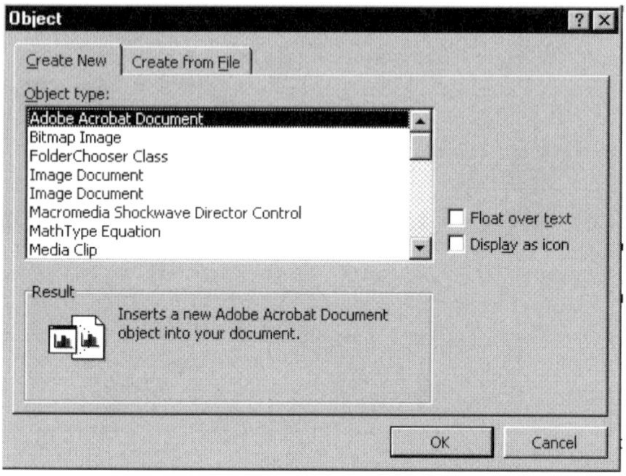

Figure 17.5a Create New tab of Insert Object window.

Here we are concerned with importing an existing application file, which will, at least in principle, continue to be updated in Excel. So we go to the second tab (Figure 17.5b), **Create from File**. This assumes that we know what we want to insert and where it is, so we browse until we find our Excel file. The text at the bottom left tells you what is going to happen. Note that there are three further options:

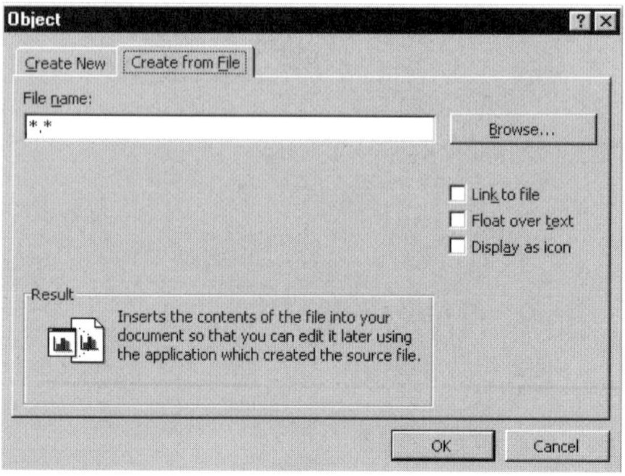

Figure 17.5b Create from File tab of Insert Object window.

★ ECDL ★

● **Link to file**: If this is not ticked, then the effect is the same as it was with
the first two methods. Figure 17.6a shows the change in the text when it is
ticked.

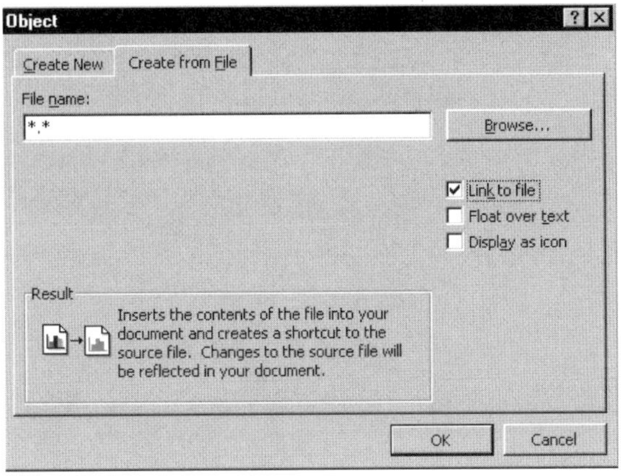

Object

Create New | Create from File

File name:
[*.*   ] | Browse...

☑ Link to file
☐ Float over text
☐ Display as icon

Result
Inserts the contents of the file into your
document and creates a shortcut to the
source file. Changes to the source file will
be reflected in your document.

[OK] [Cancel]

Figure 17.6a The text with Link to file selected.

● **Float over text**: This is the equivalent of the command we met on the
Picture menu in Chapter 16. The text does not change when this is ticked.

● **Display as icon** (Figure 17.6b): In this case, only an icon is shown in the
document. This is mainly of use if the document is not to be printed.
Clicking on the icon will open the linked document.

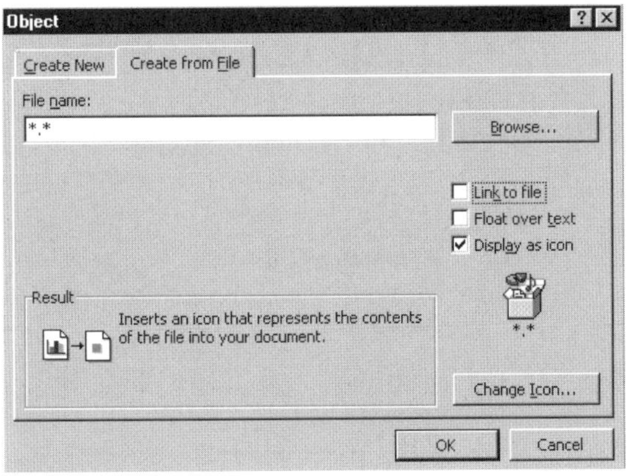

Object

Create New | Create from File

File name:
[*.*   ] | Browse...

☐ Link to file
☐ Float over text
☑ Display as icon

Result
Inserts an icon that represents the contents
of the file into your document.

[Change Icon...]

[OK] [Cancel]

Figure 17.6b The text with Display as icon selected.

You can have all or none of these options ticked.

As noted above, you can achieve the same result with the link by using **Copy** in Excel, but then, instead of using **Paste**, you use **Paste Special** from the **Edit** menu; note that there is no keyboard shortcut for **Paste Special**. There are various options that you can choose (see Figure 17.7), but these are all explained. While the principle is within the ECDL syllabus, the detail is not.

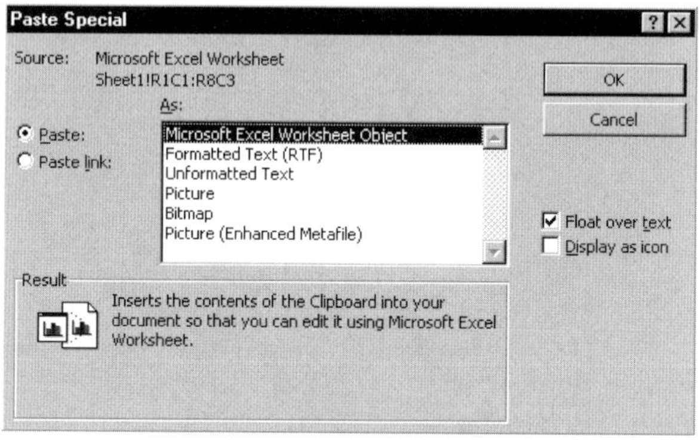

Paste Special	? X
Source: Microsoft Excel Worksheet Sheet1!R1C1:R8C3	OK
As:	Cancel

○ Paste:
○ Paste link:

Microsoft Excel Worksheet Object
Formatted Text (RTF)
Unformatted Text
Picture
Bitmap
Picture (Enhanced Metafile)

☑ Float over text
☐ Display as icon

Result
Inserts the contents of the Clipboard into your document so that you can edit it using Microsoft Excel Worksheet.

Figure 17.7 The Paste Special window.

Now repeat the first exercise in this chapter, but this time use **Insert Object**. Once you have inserted the object, click on it to edit it and watch what happens.

Repeat the first exercise in this chapter, but this time use **Paste Special** instead of just **Paste**. Once you have done this, click on it to edit it and watch what happens. It should be the same as when using the **Insert Object** option.

17.5. Pasting Charts

Within Excel, it is possible to generate charts based on the data (see Module 4 for further details) and one has been generated from the ECDL spreadsheet data (Figure 17.8). We can copy and then either **Paste** or **Paste Special** in the same way as we did above. If we do the latter, then the data in the chart is linked back to the original spreadsheet and will be updated as and when the spreadsheet is updated.

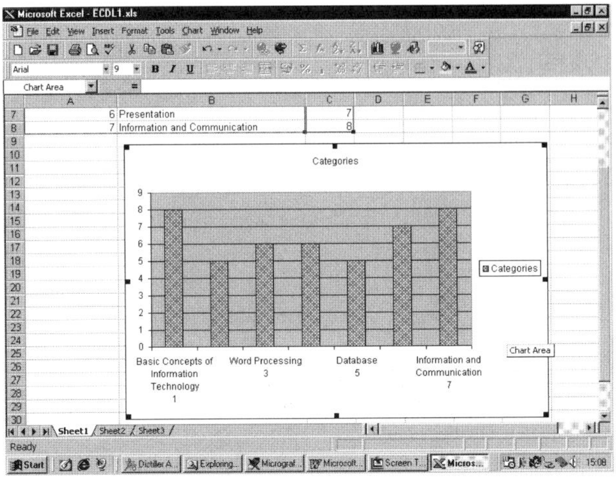

Figure 17.8 Pasting an Excel chart into Word.

Exercise 17.5

Repeat the previous exercise in this chapter, but this time, before you do that, create a chart in Excel. Then copy the chart. Once you have inserted the chart in Word, again click on it to edit it and watch what happens.

Summary

In this chapter:

● We have looked at copying and pasting a spreadsheet and a chart from Excel into Word.
● We have looked at importing a spreadsheet into Word.
● We have looked at importing objects into Word from other applications and retaining the link with the original application.
● We have looked at Paste Special for copying and pasting into Word from other applications and retaining the link with the original application.

Mail Merge

18

★ ECDL ★

18.1. Introduction

One great advantage (or disadvantage, depending on your viewpoint) of computers is that they can do things over and over again, very fast. Thus, if you have a list of names and addresses, producing an individualised letter to each person on the list is very straightforward. This is known as mail merging because the production of such letters and labels was its prime purpose. However, it can be used to for various other purposes as well; these are outside the scope of ECDL.

18.2. Creating the List

The first thing to note is that you do not necessarily have to create the list. You can, of course, and we shall see how, but in most cases the list will come from a spreadsheet, a database or a Word file in which the fields (that is the different parts of the name and address) are separated in a standard way. This might be as a table (like the one you created in Chapter 15), but it can even be what is called a delimited text file that, for example, looks like:

TitlelFirstnamelSurnamelAddress 1lTownlCountylPostcode
MrlJohnlSmithl1 Church StreetlBradfordlWest YorkslBD22 3XL
MslGlorialBrownl22 High StreetlBathlWiltslBA34 9ZZ

You will notice that there are the same number of fields in each entry and the fields are described in the top line. With many addresses that match this format (and of course many addresses do not, so the format has to be more complex in reality), we can carry out a mail merge.

Exercise 18.2

You can create the list using whatever approach you prefer. However, Word has some special routines to help you. Go to the **Tools** menu and select **Mail Merge**. The **Mail Merge Helper** in Figure 18.1a appears. The first thing you have to do is create the **Main Document**, i.e. the master letter. If you click on this you get several alternatives, **Form Letters**, **Mailing Labels**, **Envelopes** and **Catalog** (Figure 18.1b). Let us click on **Form Letters**. You can then either use your current document or create a new one. We will create a new one, which at the moment we will leave blank. We will come back to this in a moment.

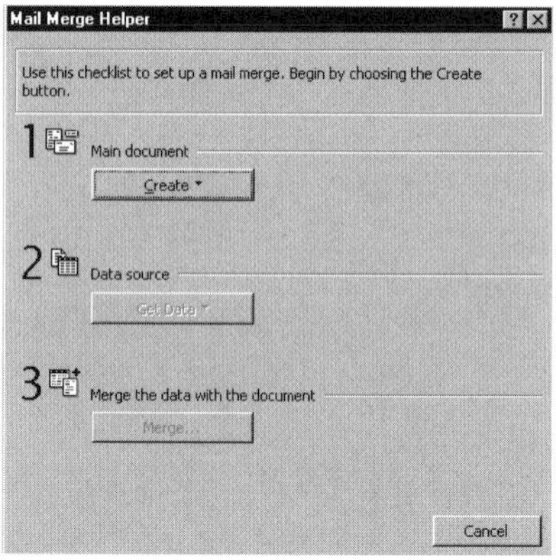

Figure 18.1a The Mail Merge Helper window.

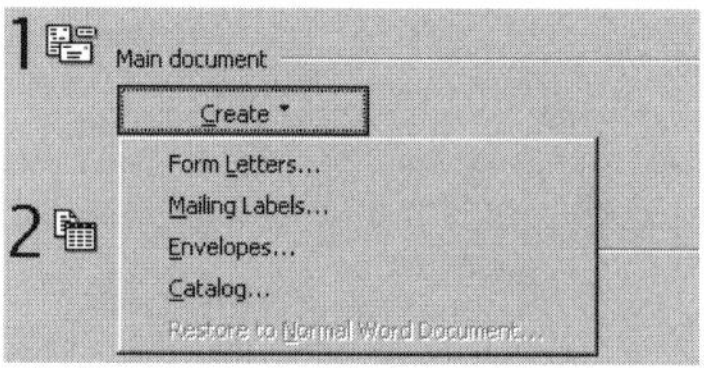

Figure 18.1b The Main document options in the Mail Merge Helper window.

Let us go back to the main Mail Merge window and move on to creating the data source. Figure 18.2 shows us that we can create a new data source or use an existing data source. There are also two other options, which use other sources, but which we will ignore. If you choose to use an existing data source like the example above, then you browse through the system in the usual way until you find the file you want and open it.

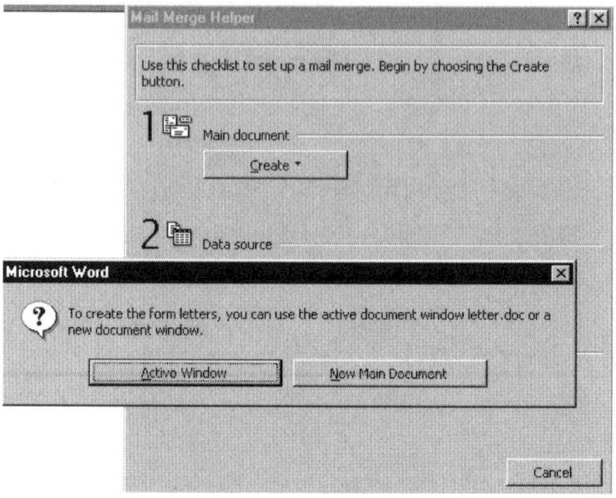

Figure 18.2 Choice of creating a data source or using an existing data source.

★ ★ ★
★ ★
★ ECDL ★
★ ★
★ ★ ᵇ

If you decide to create a data source, you then see a window like Figure 18.3, which allows you to choose the fields from a standard set that Microsoft provides. Once you are happy with that, you have to save the file. Then you see a screen into which you can enter data (Figure 18.4). You are then able to go ahead and enter data.

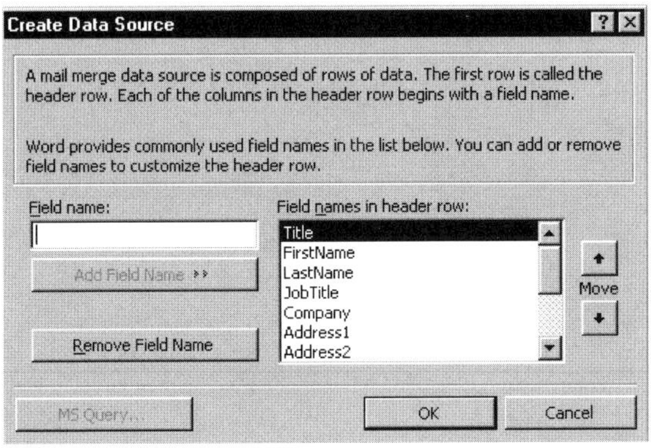

Create Data Source `?` `X`

A mail merge data source is composed of rows of data. The first row is called the header row. Each of the columns in the header row begins with a field name.

Word provides commonly used field names in the list below. You can add or remove field names to customize the header row.

Field name:

Field names in header row:

Title
FirstName
LastName
JobTitle
Company
Address1
Address2

Add Field Name ▸▸

Remove Field Name

Move ↑ ↓

MS Query...   OK   Cancel

Figure 18.3 Choosing fields for the data source.

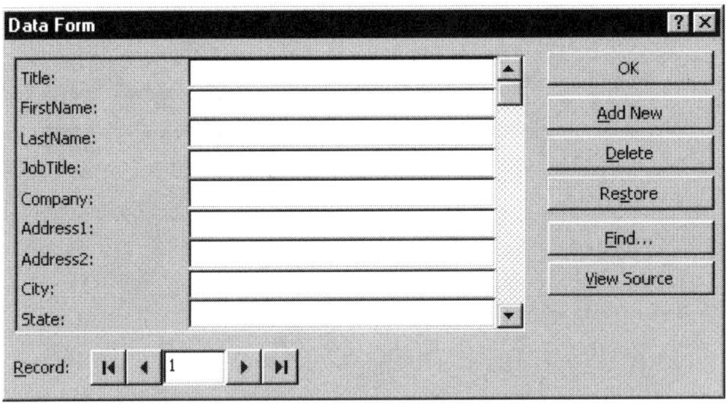

Data Form `?` `X`

Title:
FirstName:
LastName:
JobTitle:
Company:
Address1:
Address2:
City:
State:

OK
Add New
Delete
Restore
Find...
View Source

Record: |◀ ◀ 1 ▶ ▶|

Figure 18.4 The data entry screen open in Mail Merge.

18.3. Creating the Main Document

You now need to add the fields that you have created into the main document.

Exercise 18.3

When you go back to your master document, you will see that there is a box on the toolbar that allows you to enter a Merge field. This is in fact part of the **Mail Merge** toolbar, which is shown complete in Figure 18.5. Figure 18.6a shows the top of a letter with some fields entered and the drop-down menu showing how you choose the next field. Figure 18.6b shows the complete fields of the address. Once your letter is complete, you can save it. You may also see messages asking if you want to save the associated mailing list.

Figure 18.5 The Mail Merge toolbar.

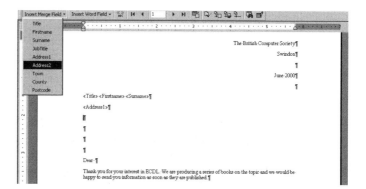

Figure 18.6a Selecting the next field for the master document from the drop-down menu.

Figure 18.6b The completed fields for the address.

Note that if you use an existing document, you enter the fields in the same way.

If, instead of producing a letter, you want to produce a set of address labels, then you choose **Mailing Labels** in Figure 18.1b and you will need to select

(or create) a file, just as for a mailing letter. We shall use the same file as we used for the letter.

You will then be told that you need to set up your main document. If you click appropriately, you will see a window (Figure 18.7a) where you can choose the type of label you want to use (to correspond to your stationery). Unfortunately, there is no preview and the file does not tell you how many labels per sheet. However, the dimensions are given and, from these, you can work out which label you need. Once you have selected an appropriate label size – and remember to select the A4 and A5 size, rather than the (US) standard – you will see a window (Figure 18.7b) that allows you to enter the merge fields (Figure 18.7c), in a similar way to that which you used for the letter. Once you have completed that, you will see the completed master document (Figure 18.7d).

information

When you first see your Main document it will appear as in Figure 18.7d. However, if you switch back to it after merging, you will find that the second and subsequent records have acquired an extra field <Next Record> (Figure 18.7e). The reason for this should be obvious.

caution!

Do not use the Envelopes and Labels option on the Tools menu. This has a somewhat different use, which is outside the scope of ECDL.

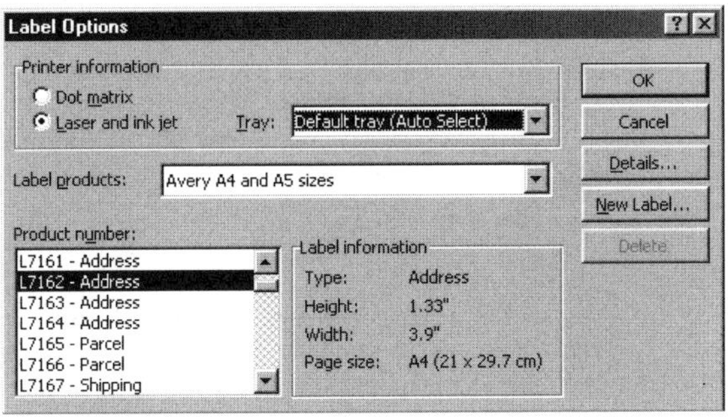

Figure 18.7a Choosing the label type.

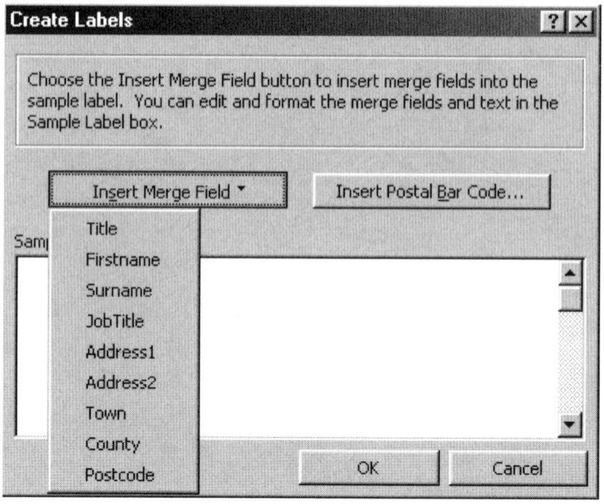

Figure 18.7b Choosing your merge fields.

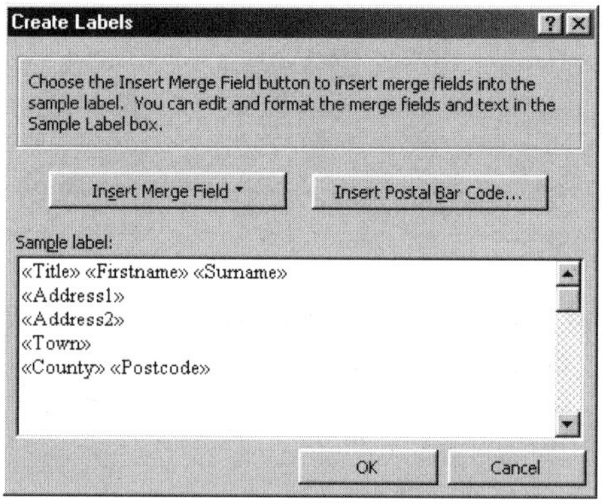

Figure 18.7c Viewing a sample label.

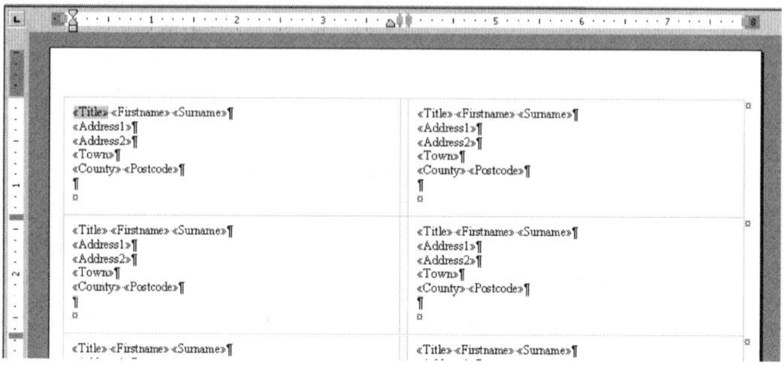

Figure 18.7d The completed main document.

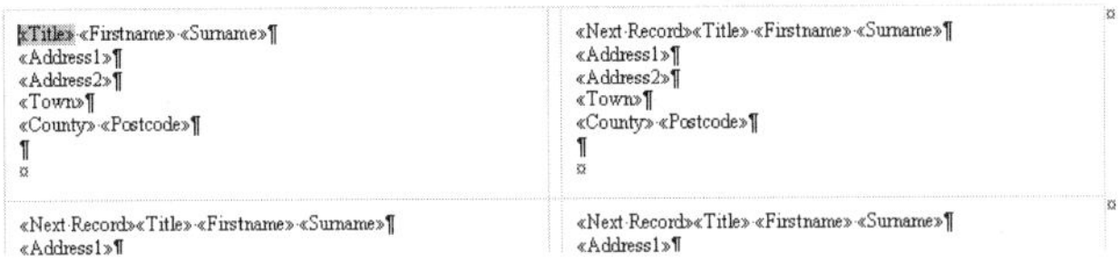

Figure 18.7e Additional <Next Record> field.

18.4. Merging

The third part of the Mail Merge Helper is the actual merge, which is carried out in the same way for both letters and labels.

Exercise 18.4a

When you click on **Merge**, you then see another dialogue box, which allows you to choose whether to merge to a new file or direct to the printer and whether to leave blanks if a field is empty (in an address, you usually do not). You can also choose which of the records you want to merge (Figure 18.8). There are also options on the toolbar for launching the merge directly and checking that the merge is doing what you want. Once you are happy, then you can launch the merge and get ready to put everything into (window) envelopes and stick on the stamps! Of course, if you have also created labels, you can use these instead of window envelopes!

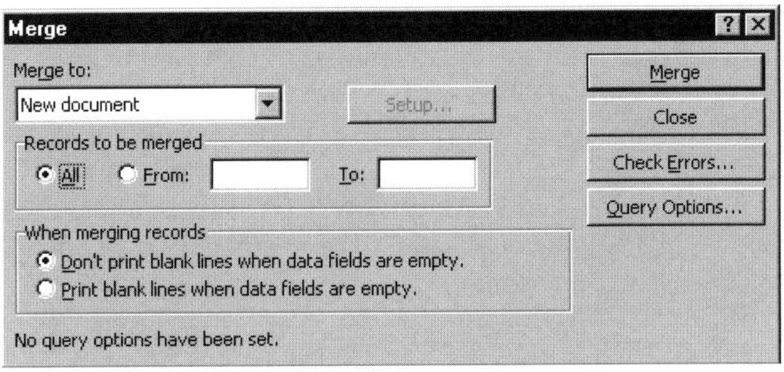

Figure 18.8 Deciding which records to merge.

Exercise 18.4b

1. Open your letter file. Select **Mail Merge** from the **Tools** menu and select **Create** for the main document and then **Form Letters**.

2. Then you will be given the option to choose between the **Active Window** (your letter) and a new file. While you can choose to create a new file, we suggest that you click on **Active Window** to use your letter.

step **3.** You then need to create a data source. Again you can choose to **Create a data source**, but again, we suggest that you use the table file that you created earlier. You will need to browse and then open it.

step **4.** You will now see a message that tells you that there are no fields in your main document and then gives you the chance to edit that document. Click on **Edit Main Document**.

step **5.** You will now see on your **Mail Merge** toolbar **Insert Merge Field**. Place the text cursor where you want a field and select one (you use the down arrow as usual to see them).

step **6.** When you have inserted the fields you can save (better to save as a new file) and then run your merge by clicking the merge icon [icon]. You will then see a window like Figure 18.8.

step **7.** Try the different options and then click **Merge** (to a New document). You can always delete that file and merge again.

Exercise 18.4c

step **1.** Select **Mail Merge** from the **Tools** menu and select **Create** for the main document and then **Mailing Labels**.

step **2.** As in the previous exercise, you will be given the option to choose between the Active Window (the new file) and a new file. In this case, choose a new file.

step **3.** You then need to create or open your data source. Again use the table file that you created earlier. As in the previous exercise, you will need to browse and then open it.

step **4.** You will now see a message that tells you that you need to set up your main document. If you click appropriately, you can then select the label size (and layout) that you want to use. Note that the label size for 21 to a sheet is 63.5 by 38.1 mm and for 14 to a sheet the size is 99.1 by 38.1 mm.

step **5.** Once you have selected the size of label, you enter the data fields and click OK when you have finished. You will see your label document.

step **6.** Run merge from the toolbar **Merge** icon. You will then see a window, as in Figure 18.8.

step 7. Try the different options and then click Merge (in the first instance to a new document but you can later merge directly to the printer). If you do merge directly to the printer, it is a good idea to ensure that you have put in the label stationery!

Note that you can also access the **Mail Merge Helper** from icon .

You can access the data entry (in which you can check, modify your data file) from icon ▦. You can, as always, identify the icons by mousing over them.

Summary

In this chapter:

● We have looked at the idea of mail merging.
● We have seen how to set up a mail merge.

Index

★ ★ ★
★ ECDL ★
★ ★ ꜜ

★ ECDL ★

★ ECDL ★

European Computer Driving Licence™

the european pc skills standard

★★★ ®
★ ★
★ ECDL ★
★ ★
★ ★ ★

Springer's study guides have been designed to complement the ECDL syllabus, and be consistent with the content contained within it. Each study guide enables you to successfully complete the European Driving Licence (ECDL). The books cover a range of specific knowledge areas and skill sets, with clearly defined learning objectives, broken down into seven modules.

Each module has been written in clear, jargon-free language, with self-paced exercises and regular review questions, to help prepare you for ECDL Tests.

Titles in the series include:

- **Module 1: Basic Concepts of Information Technology**
  ISBN: 1-85233-442-8   Softcover   £9.95

- **Module 2: Using the Computer & Managing Files**
  ISBN: 1-85233-443-6   Softcover   £9.95

- **Module 3: Word Processing**
  ISBN: 1-85233-444-4   Softcover   £9.95

- **Module 4: Spreadsheets**
  ISBN: 1-85233-445-2   Softcover   £9.95

- **Module 5: Database**
  ISBN: 1-85233-446-0   Softcover   £9.95

- **Module 6: Presentation**
  ISBN: 1-85233-447-9   Softcover   £9.95

- **Module 7: Information & Communication**
  ISBN: 1-85233-448-7   Softcover   £9.95

All books are available, of course, from all good booksellers (who can order them even if they are not in stock), but if you have difficulties you can contact the publisher direct by telephoning +44 (0) 1483 418822 or by emailing orders@svl.co.uk

For details of other Springer books and journals, please visit

www.springer.de